DENTAL PRACTICE TRANSITIONS HANDBOOK

An Insider's Guide to Buying, Selling, Associates, and Partnerships

H. M. Smith, MBA

ADS Florida / Professional Transitions

Dental Practice Transitions Handbook: An Insider's Guide to Buying, Selling, Associates, and Partnerships

Published by Wheatmark®
610 East Delano Street, Suite 104
Tucson, Arizona 85705 U.S.A.
www.wheatmark.com

International Standard Book Number: 978-1-60494-526-3
Library of Congress Control Number: 2010930448

Contents

Foreword

Any transition activity—buying, selling, or associating in a professional practice—is one of the most important events that will happen in your professional career. Making a mistake in the process can have long-lasting effects on any or all of the parties to a transition.

I first wrote *Buying or Selling a Professional Practice* in 1990 to give a brief overview of issues that I felt a buyer or seller should be aware of, or at least consider, when buying or selling a dental practice. In 2005, I updated and revised the original book to make the information current with the marketplace at that time. Now, twenty years since my first edition, much has changed in the arena of professional practice transitions and dentistry itself. In every way, dentistry has changed dramatically. The marketplace has changed as well, and in the thirty-five-plus years that I have been consulting with dentists, there is little that has remained constant.

I would like to thank those who have contributed to my education and understanding of sound ethical and fundamental principles that I have tried to apply and convey to clients in order to assist them in the decision-making process when considering transition issues. Amy Morgan and her team at Pride Institute have provided knowledge of management skills; Bill Prescott, Esq., provides support with legal and tax issues. My colleagues at ADS continue to be the best in the industry in advising dentists throughout the country on transition issues. And certainly my immediate associates at ADS Florida and Professional Transitions, Stuart Auerbach, DDS; Paul Rang, DMD, JD; and Gregory Auerbach, MBA, continue to be the best.

Hopefully, this handbook will provide you with the answers to basic questions when considering any transition. It is not intended to replace the experts, brokers, consultants, attorneys, accountants, and financial advisors that should be consulted as you proceed through a transition, but it should give you an understanding of the process and what to expect and a starting point from which to begin your journey.

Demographics in Dentistry

'Tis not knowing much, but what is useful,
that makes a wise man.

THOMAS FULLER

To understand where dentistry has been and where it is going, it is important to understand how dentistry has changed and what to expect.

Entering the twenty-first century, the largest number of baby boomer dentists is approaching retirement. The seventies, eighties, and early nineties produced the most dentists in history. Dental schools had opened throughout the country, and then in the mid-nineties, 10% of the dental schools closed because of an oversupply of dentists.

That oversupply changed dentistry forever. Dentists became competitive through advertising and marketing methods that had never been accepted in the profession before. Insurance companies decided that they could and would take advantage of the competitive marketplace and threatened "a dental practice in every Sears store," saying, "If you don't join us, you will be left behind."

Fortunately, the dental community stood its ground and, for the most part, rejected the premise that reduced fees through the control of the insurance industry was the future. Unfortunately, the medical community collapsed, and medical practitioners became the victims of big insurance and most likely will never recover.

During the same period, advances in technology and materials propelled dentistry from a necessity of maintenance to a desire for a beautiful smile. Bleaching, composite materials, orthodontics, and implants replaced yellow, uneven teeth with silver fillings, or worse, dentures. The media marketed a beautiful smile, and dentists were all too willing to provide the expertise necessary.

Before the influx of dentists, there were approximately 1,800 patients per dentist in America. That number dropped below 1,000 at the peak output of dental

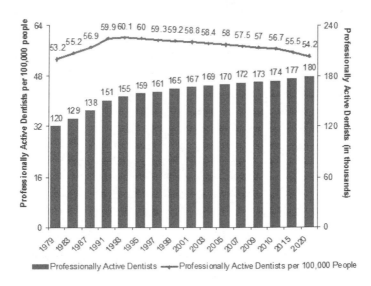

Graph 1

schools that created the competitive environment. As schools closed and fewer dentists graduated, the numbers reversed, and presently we see approximately 2,300 patients per dentist, a number that is growing nationwide. See Graph #1

The only statistic that may also impact the supply of and demand for dentists is that 50% or more of the dental students graduating are female. This is not a bad thing in any way, but there is some question about whether female dentists will practice the same career hours as their male counterparts. If, in fact, they do not, it will continue to put pressure on the profession as the demand for dentistry continues to increase (see demographic graphs). See Graph #2

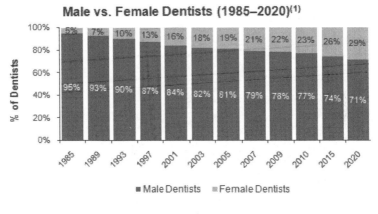

Graph 2

In addition, dentists are in demand to provide that perfect smile, and Americans are oral-health aware. Everyone wants a healthy mouth and pretty smile, and many are willing to pay whatever it costs.

Presently, we see fewer dentists graduating, more den-

tists retiring, the population growing, and more patients
who need and want dental health care. See Graph #3

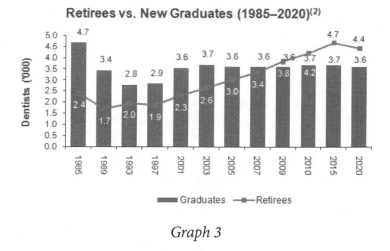

Graph 3

So how does this information affect buyers and sellers? If there are more dentists retiring than those seeking
a practice, we find ourselves in a buyer's market. A buyer's
market depresses prices because there is more product on
the market than can be sold. It also creates an environment
for starting from scratch if the competition in a market
does not exist. This is especially true with the specialties
in dentistry. On the other hand, if there are few practices
for sale and a lot of buyers in a market, there is a seller's
market because fewer opportunities exist, and buyers are
willing to pay more for those that do.

These buyer's or seller's markets are demographic-
specific. One market may be a buyer's market because of
a large number of retiring dentists, whereas another area
may be a seller's market because of economic issues or a
lack of retiring dentists compared to those looking to buy.

When looking to buy or sell, consider the demographic issues of your specific location. Is it a growing community or struggling economically? Is there a need for more dentists in the community or fewer? Analyzing this information will help you understand what you can expect regarding the time it will take to find or sell a practice, how much you can expect to receive or pay for a practice, and whether it makes sense to consider starting from scratch as a potential buyer or walking away without selling as a seller.

The good news is that the pendulum is swinging in favor of dentistry: more demand, less supply. The concern is that if the public is not provided adequate dental care because of the lack of dentists available, it is likely and can be expected that the government—federal or state—may legislate some adjustment in supply to accommodate the need. This could include the opening of more dental schools, reducing the standards required to perform certain procedures with expanded-duty technicians, or having less stringent licensing for foreign-trained dentists.

All of these issues together create an interesting environment for both the retiring dentist and the new dentist. It also creates a very exciting future for dentistry. Hopefully, it will be positive, productive, and economically beneficial to both buyers and sellers and to the public at large.

Determining Practice Value

*Many terms are used to define value ... Only a few of these
have some definition. Others have the definition which the
parties choose to place upon them.*

JOHN E. MOYE, ESQ.

Determining the value of a dental practice is as critical
to the seller as it is to the buyer. In this chapter, we will
try to provide an overview of the methods of valuation,
the valuation process, and the criteria accepted by the professional appraisal community.

The value of an item is never determined until someone actually pays for it. How often have we heard of a
famous art work expected to sell at a certain price and
actually selling for much more or much less than anticipated? An item can have an *asking price* or an *estimated
value*, but the actual value is determined when the money
changes hands. This is also true for a dental practice. The
asking price is what a seller would like to receive, the offering price is what a buyer is willing to pay, and the ap-

praised value is what an appraiser provides as an educated opinion of value.

Several terms that we should clearly understand are:

Price—the amount asked by the seller
Cost—the amount paid by the buyer
Value—the amount paid by the buyer to the seller

The Internal Revenue Service, through revenue rulings and litigated settlements and agreements, has defined *fair market value* as "the price at which the property would change hands between a willing buyer and a willing seller when the former is not under any compulsion to buy, and the latter is not under any compulsion to sell, both parties having reasonable knowledge of the relevant facts" (Revenue Ruling 65-180).

In common parlance, we refer to fair market value as *"willing buyer, willing seller."* This is very important because until we have a willing buyer and a willing seller, we don't have a deal. As important as willing buyer and willing seller are, the other very important elements of Revenue Ruling 65-180 are that "neither party is under any compulsion and that both parties have reasonable knowledge of the relevant facts."

The compulsion issue stands alone. There are rare situations where death, disability, or some other event can cause the seller to be under pressure to sell, but pressure is *not* compulsion.

On the other hand, having knowledge of the relevant facts is another issue entirely. This is where a valid appraisal performed by a qualified appraiser using legitimate and accepted appraisal methods is critical.

It is also where the buyer and seller perform their own due diligence and take some of the responsibility of understanding the implications of entering into a transaction. A legitimate appraisal with explanations and justifications will greatly assist both parties in making these assessments.

There is a big difference between facts and feelings. Facts are information in the form of data that can be written, verified, and replicated. Feelings, on the other hand, are just that. One person may feel a particular way, and another person may feel an entirely different way. Both feelings and facts are important in the decision-making process, and neither should be less valuable when establishing a selling price for a seller or analyzing a practice to buy by a purchaser. If the data are not there or suggest a deficiency in the practice, that fact must be reflected in the value. If the feeling is not there, it may not be reflected in the offer by the buyer. One buyer may feel warm and fuzzy whereas another may not.

Feelings are subjective, so we will leave the feelings out of the analysis process. Suffice it to say, if a buyer does not have a good feeling, he or she probably will not buy.

Since facts and data are objective, we can look at the numbers and analyze, compare, and project to help us to arrive at a value. But the numbers are only one component of value. The other component is risk.

Value is a function of net income and risk.

Risk is the subjective component to the process of appraising in contrast to the numbers, which are objective. What is important to understand is that without the objective component, there can be no knowledge of the relevant facts, and without the subjective component, there is limited reasonable knowledge.

Without getting into the complexities of the different processes used in valuing professional practices, it is possible to review, in a generalized manner, the methods used and the information required to perform an appraisal. The terms *appraisal, valuation,* and *opinion of value* may be interchanged; however, it should be noted that an appraisal usually suggests a written report justifying the opinion of value, supported by data collected and applied by the appraiser. It is important to note, though, that an appraisal or opinion of value may be verbal as well. The important thing to remember is that to be considered an appraisal, certain specific information about the subject property has to be known and analyzed. If an opinion of value is made without the necessary information, the representation of value is most likely the result of using a *rule of thumb*. A rule of thumb is a generalized estimation that may not be precise or, for that matter, even representative of actual value.

An example of a rule of thumb is: "A practice is worth 65% of gross income."

To show that this is not a valid opinion of value, let's look at two practices, each grossing $800,000. Using the rule of thumb, both practices would be worth $520,000. However, if one practice has an overhead of 50% with the dentist taking home $400,000 and the other practice has an overhead of 70% with the doctor taking home $240,000, are they equal in value? Of course not! (We will discuss what constitutes actual overhead in the chapter on systems.) The missing information includes the relevant facts relating to the expenses of the practice.

Another example is using the same practices with $800,000 in gross production and both having an equal

50% overhead, but one has all new, state-of-the-art equipment and the other has old, outdated equipment. Again, these two practices are certainly worth different amounts, even though they provide the same amount of income to the dentists.

Knowledge of the relevant facts suggests that the information is available and has been analyzed correctly. To achieve a proper analysis, it only makes sense that someone who is qualified to do the analysis does the analysis. It would not be appropriate for an attorney to diagnose and suggest a treatment plan to a dental patient, nor would it be appropriate for a dentist to interpret the law.

The government has established standards that should be met when an appraisal is performed. The Uniform Standard of Professional Appraisal Practice (USPAP) outlines the performance standards and practices that should be followed and adhered to whenever an appraisal is performed. If the person or firm performing an appraisal does not adhere to the USPAP standards, there will be no assurance that the relevant facts and information have been analyzed and interpreted properly. In addition to USPAP, the Institute of Business Appraisers (IBA) and the American Society of Appraisers (ASA) have established standards and certifications for appraisals and appraisers. One of the standards that is universally accepted and required by all organizations is that the appraiser be knowledgeable in the area of the appraisal. This means that if you are engaging an appraiser to place a value on a dental practice, that appraiser must have knowledge about dental practices. This is one weakness that I see in the appraisal community: some appraisers accept an assignment to value a business that they know nothing about.

I often see appraisals that have been performed by accountants or consultants who do not follow the USPAP, ASA or IBA standards. The value arrived at may or may not be reasonable, but the method, analysis, and replication have to be questioned.

So what are the methods of valuation? There are two universally accepted approaches for valuing dental practices. The first is the ~~market approach.~~ The market approach to value ~~uses comparable previous sales of like practices to determine value~~, much the same as real estate appraisals use comparable sales of real estate to establish value. This approach is ~~the most accurate and most defendable method of valuation.~~ It is hard to argue that like practices do not have reasonably like values. The following chart shows over two thousand data points, each representing the sale of a dental practice.[1]

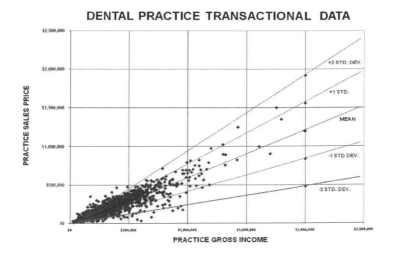

DENTAL PRACTICE TRANSACTIONAL DATA

It is information such as the above that provides us with the ability to compare a proposed value to that of other transactions in order to confirm that the value arrived at using other methods of valuation falls within the reasonable parameters of the market place. It is also information, such as the above, that allows rules of thumb to be used or misused instead of using legitimate appraisal methods. It is easy to use the market data and derive a percentage of gross as the going market value, when, in fact, the previous examples show how other factors impact the actual value of the practice.

The second universally accepted method of valuation is the capitalization of earnings approach. The capitalization of earnings approach uses the concept that a multiple of earnings or the capitalization of earnings represents a legitimate return on investment and therefore a legitimate value. Capitalization converts earnings or excess income to value. The problem that has to be solved is, what are earnings? In a dental practice, the earnings are always distributed to the owner(s). Therefore, no earnings are identified, and with no earnings, there is no value. To address this, it is necessary to analyze and adjust the income and expense statement to determine the actual required expenses that are necessary to operate the practice and the usual and customary salary that would be paid to a dentist if he or she were to be hired to perform the dentistry in the practice. In most cases, this will result in some income left over that can be capitalized. This process requires someone with knowledge of dental practice management, industry standard expense norms, and acceptable salary ranges to do the analysis.

Once a true net income has been arrived at by analyzing and adjusting the income and expense statement to reflect real practice income and expenses, we have to apply the risk factors that impact value. As stated before, value is a function of net income and risk. Risk factors include many things, such as local and national economic conditions, age and condition of equipment, location, types of procedures, staff competence and experience, size of the practice, percentages of managed care and reduced fee dentistry, specialties and specialty procedures in a general dental office, location, facility lease conditions, and practice systems.

Practice systems reflect the management and transferability of the practice. Systems consist of scheduling, number of active and new patients, charting, recall, and accounts receivable management. All of these issues need to be analyzed and the risk associated with them determined before a value can be arrived at. We will discuss systems in a later chapter, but for now, accept that if the systems in a practice are not functioning properly, a buyer is less likely to want to purchase the practice, or will pay less for it. As such, a disorganized practice would lend to the point that higher risk yields lower value.

The size of a practice can also be a risk factor. If the practice is grossing less than $300,000 per year, it is likely that there will be little, if anything, left for a buyer after the operating expenses and the debt service (payments for the money borrowed to purchase the practice) have been paid. Not many buyers are willing to buy a practice if they cannot take home a reasonable salary.

Example:

Practice gross income	$300,000
Actual operating overhead 65%	– $195,000
Net income	$105,000

Annual debt service for $195,000 purchase Price (65% of gross) amortized over 7 years At 7% interest	– $ 35,317
Net take home before taxes	$ 69,683

Considering taxes will still need to be paid on the earnings, it would be hard to live on less than $70,000, raise a family and pay off school loans. Because of this, the commercial lenders are reluctant to finance a practice purchase where the take home is so low even if a purchaser is willing to buy.

On the other hand, a practice grossing $1,200,000 or more requires an experienced clinician and administrator. This experience is not readily available in most new buyers, thus once again creating greater risk in selling the practice.

Because fewer and fewer specialists (as a ratio of the population) are graduating, it has become easy in many locations to start up a practice from scratch, reducing the available buyers, and thus creating a greater risk of selling a specialty practice.

Specialties within a general practice also create risk. For example, if a practice has a significant portion of the production generated by a specialty such as TMJ or orthodontics, it is hard to find a buyer who is qualified and has the same philosophical approach to the specialty as the seller. The same issue exists for any specialty practiced within a general practice, including pediatric dentistry, endodontics, implant surgery, and periodontics (usually large soft-tissue management programs).

If, in fact, there is significant specialty practiced within a general practice, the portion of revenue generated by the specialty may have to be carved out of the gross production, thus reducing the gross production and concurrently net income to the practice, thereby lowering the value.

The liquidity of money is usually determined by the prime interest rate, the cost of borrowing money (lending fees), treasury notes and bonds, and T-bill rates. The reason these are used in the appraisal analysis when considering risk is to provide a comparison to the risk of investing money in something other than a risk-free instrument. Treasury instruments are considered risk-free because the government would have to collapse for a default to occur. So, if by investing in a dental practice, the return on investment (ROI) is equal to or less than putting the same money into a Treasury instrument, it would be foolish to invest in the dental practice. The converse is also true, however, that if investing in a dental practice the return is greater than putting money into a Treasury instrument, then the risk can be justified.

All of the above factors need to be evaluated in order to develop a capitalization rate (cap rate). This number is properly arrived at by what is called the build-up method. The build-up method takes into consideration all of the risk factors and builds them up to a percentage number that is used as a denominator which is divided into the adjusted net income (the numerator) with the resulting number as the value.

The discussion of this process is not intended to educate in order that anyone can perform an appraisal, but more to advise that there is a very defined process that is accepted by the financial community and the legal system that complies with USPAP, ASA and IBA standards for appraisers to be used in determining the value of a dental practice.

Other methods that are common to the appraisals of other businesses and industries, but are not usually appropriate for dentistry are the discounted future earnings approach, the amortization of earnings approach and the asset summation approach.

Discounted future earnings (sometimes referred to as multiple period discounting approach) assumes continued performance of the practice based on previous historical data and the projection of that performance. This is certainly appropriate for businesses that do not change in character from one owner to another, such as a supermarket or gas station. Obviously, in every dental practice transition, the practice changes with the change in dentists.

The amortization of earnings method is used primarily for big industry that has capitalized assets primarily responsible for generating the income, such as the automobile assembly plant where large robots and conveyer belts do the work that generate the money.

The asset summation approach determines the value of each of the assets, equipment, supplies, furnishings, accounts receivable, goodwill, and so forth and adds them all together to arrive at a value. In the sale of a dental practice, the assumption is that all of the assets work together to arrive at a value.

While these approaches may not be specifically appropriate, they are, most often, calculated and analyzed in conjunction with the values determined by the market and cap rate approaches.

All of this information is provided to communicate that there is a formal process accepted by the professional communities for determining a practice value. If these accepted practices and processes are not used, the asking price by the seller or the offering price proffered by the buyer may not have any basis of support and, most likely, cannot be justified.

Definitions of Value

What is being sold or bought when ownership of a dental practice is transferred from a seller to a buyer?

Primarily, the buyer is purchasing a stream of revenue or cash flow. This cash flow is generated in a dental practice by the skill and expertise (intangible assets or goodwill) of the dentist and his team using equipment and supplies (tangible assets).

The purchase of any business, including a dental practice, usually includes the transfer of ownership of the tangible assets and the intangible assets or goodwill.

Tangible assets include the equipment, supplies, merchandise, accounts receivable, and the leasehold improvements. The equipment is usually the least valuable component of the practice value as it can be replaced at a small fraction of the total practice value. Very often, buyers obsess on the equipment, when, in fact, they should be focusing on the goodwill. Tangible assets are usually reasonably easy to value and there are several approaches used:

Liquidation value is the value of the tangible assets if

they were sold to the highest bidder at auction. Returning to our willing buyer/willing seller fair market value definition, this would most likely be a sale under compulsion or forced, for some reason, to sell. Because this is not a willing buyer or willing seller environment, liquidation value is rarely used in the valuation of a dental practice.

Replacement value is the cost of replacing a piece of equipment with another piece of equipment used for the same purpose. In many cases, equipment may not be replaceable without upgrading to a newer model or newer technology. The existing equipment may be functional but not replaceable. Again, this method of valuing tangible assets is not used because it does not reflect what a willing buyer would pay for a piece of existing used equipment.

Fair market value, as we have discussed, is what a willing buyer would pay a willing seller for the tangible assets. This is usually a value that can be ascertained by a qualified dental equipment salesperson because they engage in the purchase and sale of similar equipment as a matter of everyday business.

When using the capitalization of earnings approach or the market approach to determine value, the tangible asset value is included and assumed a part of the total practice value. When using either of the above approaches, adjustments are made (as a function of greater or less risk) to account for old, out-of-date equipment or new and state-of-the-art equipment. If specialized equipment such as CEREC®, microscopes, or lasers are part of the sale, consideration is given when building up the cap rate to account for the greater or less risk attributable to this equipment. It is also important when reviewing expenses to relate certain equipment to expense norms. An example would be for a practice that uses CEREC® to have outside lab expenses significantly lower than normal, thus increasing the net income. If this is the case and additional credit is added to the value of the practice for the CEREC®, it may compound the value when, in fact, it had been taken into consideration when adjusting the expense statement. It is issues such as these where the subjectivity of the appraiser comes into play and where the experience and knowledge of dentistry and dental practices pays off. Someone without this expertise could not make the appropriate adjustments in order to arrive at a legitimate value.

The intangible assets (goodwill) are usually the most valuable component of a dental practice. Goodwill is "the difference between an established successful business and one that has yet to establish itself and achieve success."[2] Success is measured, in large part, by the money that a business generates. The intangible assets consist of, in part, reputation, name, location, systems, and in the case of specialty practices, the referral community. Because goodwill is so subjective by nature, it is necessary to back into a value using very basic algebra. If two components of an equation are known, the third can be found. Therefore:

$$\text{Tangible Assets} + \text{Intangible Assets} = \text{Value}$$
or
$$\text{Value} - \text{Tangible Assets} = \text{Intangible Assets}$$

The value of the tangible assets can be determined by requesting the equipment salesperson to provide a fair market value of the equipment and furnishings in the office. Most will provide this service at no or very little charge.

It has already been determined that by using one or both of the acceptable valuation methods— the market approach or the capitalization of earnings approach—the value of the whole practice can be determined. Therefore, if the value of the tangible assets as provided by the dental supply person is subtracted from the value arrived at for the whole practice, the remainder is the value of the goodwill. It is important to define these two values, as it will be shown later that the tax consequences to both seller and buyer are determined by the values allocated to each component.

Establishing a practice value by using the capitalization of earnings and/or market approach and determining the tangible and intangible asset values can now be used to determine whether the value arrived at makes practical sense for a purchaser.

At this point, several assumptions are made. First, it is assumed that the purchaser is buying an investment business and is not going to actually perform the dentistry, but will hire a dentist at going market rates to run the practice. Second, to make this investment, the purchaser will expect a reasonable return on investment (ROI). To make these determinations, it is important to understand the concept of cash flow.

Cash flow consists of three primary elements. The gross revenue generated in the practice has to:

1. pay the operating overhead of the practice

2. pay the debt service (the money borrowed to buy the practice)

3. pay a reasonable income and/or return on investment to the buyer

If the revenue generated by the practice does not satisfactorily meet the above criteria, it is said that the practice does not cash flow. This is a critical element when it comes to a purchaser seeking financing for the purchase of the practice. If the practice does not meet the cash flow requirements of the lender, financing for the practice will not be available.

This is another test of the value of the practice being reasonable:

If the practice does not cash flow, either the price is too high, the revenue stream or income too low, the expenses too excessive, or a combination of the above.

Once again, a legitimate appraisal will not place a value on a practice that will be outside of the accepted market values or one that will not cash flow. If either of these exist, careful scrutiny of the practice and the appraisal should be undertaken.

Unfortunately, there are brokers and consultants who will tell a seller what he or she wants to hear about value in order to get the dentist to agree to use their services to sell the practice. There are also lenders who will extend the payment terms in order to get it to cash flow. (Any purchase price will work if the payment term is long enough!) However, most legitimate lenders will identify the flawed value and not grant a loan. Further, most accountants will be able to identify cash flow problems and alert their clients to the problem. Most buyers who have been shopping for a practice are reasonably aware of what the market is doing and will not be lured into a bad deal, unless there is gross misrepresentation that is hidden or difficult to discover.

In summary, it is very possible to legitimately determine the value of a dental practice. To do this, there are two accepted and legitimate methods, the market approach and the capitalization of earnings approach, which, when determined, represent the value of the whole practice. If these methods are used correctly by skilled appraisers, the value of the practice arrived at in the appraisal will cash flow.

One thing that should be mentioned is that when interest rates are very high or very low, or net income in a practice is very high or very low, the impact on the build-up method to arrive at a cap rate will force the practice value out of the market range. Therefore, the true test of value is always the question, "Does the value fall within the market range, and does the practice cash flow at the appraised value?" That question brings us full circle to: "Will a buyer buy and will a seller sell if both have reasonable knowledge of the relevant facts?"

Systems as Risk Factors

Since looking at the risk factors in a practice is critical in determining the value of a practice (remember the higher the risk, the lower the value and inversely, the lower the risk, the higher the value), it is important to look at the various systems in a practice and determine if and how they would create more or less risk. A qualified appraiser is going to examine and evaluate each of the following systems to determine if the system is functioning well and if it is transferable to a potential buyer or if it poses a risk because it does not function properly.

Buyers are going to evaluate a practice and be interested or not based on how well the practice runs and whether they can take over the practice and continue its operation successfully.

SCHEDULING—Scheduling properly is one of the most demanding responsibilities the front office staff has. Very often, it is done haphazardly without any framework or structure. If done improperly, it not only contributes to a disorganized and chaotic practice, but costs the practice significant potential income while reducing the productivity of the dentist and his hygiene staff.

The most effective schedule is one that is *pre-blocked*. That is to say, blocks of time are pre-scheduled each day for procedures or production goals. This process begins by preparing an annual plan for the practice. An annual plan projects the anticipated or desired gross revenue, the legitimate overhead costs, the retirement contribution, and the compensation before taxes for the dentist. Once these numbers have been determined, it is necessary to decide the number of working days per year. Vacation, holidays, and weekends need to be taken into consideration. With this information, it is possible to back into a per-day production number. The following is an example of how to establish a daily production goal number:

Dentist production	$ 770,000
Hygiene production	$ 230,000
Practice gross income projection	$1,000,000
Practice operating overhead	$ 600,000
Dr. pre-tax income including retirement contribution	$ 400,000

Total working days per year: 190

So, to produce $1,000,000 on four days per week working 190 days, the daily production goal would be:

Dentist	$4,053 per day
Hygiene department	$1,210 per day

For an eight-hour day, the dentist would need to have production blocks of $507 per hour, and hygiene would need to produce $151 per hour.

Obviously, every hour is not going to be scheduled for these exact amounts of time, but the hours can be scheduled in blocks. For example, a two-crown prep procedure producing $2,000 can be blocked in an hour with the expectation that the seating of the crowns will take another forty-five minutes or so but will not generate any additional income.

Several of the better dental software programs are set up for block scheduling but are rarely used properly. It is worthwhile training the schedulers in the office to use the programs properly, but to do so, realistic goals need to be set that are based on well-thought-out annual planning. Proper scheduling will reduce chaos and generate optimum revenue without running the dentist and staff ragged in the process.

OVERHEAD CONTROL—Overhead control is one of the most overlooked systems in dentistry. The first step in overhead control is to know what the required expenses in running the practice are. There are three basic categories of expenses:

1. fixed expenses

2. variable expenses

3. discretionary expenses

Fixed expenses, for the purposes of a dental office, are those required expenses that remain relatively stable regardless of the production levels of the practice. Obviously, as the practice reaches certain plateaus, the fixed expenses will change, until another plateau is reached. Fixed expenses include staff, facility, insurance, marketing, telephone, accounting, legal, and so on. All of these expenses should remain constant within ranges of production. In business terms, these are not truly fixed, but are, instead, step-expenses, but due to the nature of the dental practice, we can assume them to be very close to fixed.

Variable expenses are going to increase and decrease as a function of production (not collection). Variable expenses are limited to laboratory and supplies. In some cases where hygienists are paid a percentage of their production (which is not recommended), their pay will also qualify as a variable expense. Remember, the same expense is incurred whether you get paid or not, whether you get usual and customary (UCR) fee or a reduced fee. You are not going to use an inferior lab when providing dentistry to a reduced-fee patient. Therefore, the difference will come right out of your pocket, reducing your net income.

Discretionary expenses are those expenses that are not required to run the practice but may be desired for one reason or another. Discretionary expenses would include all of the toys that are purchased (usually spontaneously), debt service (although necessary, it is also considered discretionary because it is contributing to the equity of the owner), employee benefits, continuing education (other than that required), gifts, contributions, and automobile expenses.

Expenses can also be broken down into range norms:

Major expenses— 45% to 65% of production. (Remember, expenses remain the same whether you reduce fees, collect the money or not!)

Major expenses include:

Employees	24% to 35%
Rent	3% to 7%
Laboratory	8% to 12%
Supplies	5% to 7%

Minor expenses—10% to 14% of production.

Minor expenses include all expenses that are less than 2% of production.

Insurance
Utilities
Telephone
Dues and subscriptions
Bank charges

Discretionary expenses— Less than 10% of production.

Discretionary expenses include:

Employee benefits
Automobile expenses
Continuing education in the Bahamas

This should leave between 25% and 45% as earnings before owner's compensation (EBOC). This is the owner's pre-tax take home pay.

It is critical when running a successful business to understand and control overhead. Once each expense is placed in a category, it is then easy to create a budget that will allow control of the expenses and realistically project the expected income from the practice.

ACCOUNTS RECEIVABLE—Accounts receivable (A/R) are a tell-tale system to determine how well the patients are trained. If accounts receivable are unwieldy and delinquent, it will be obvious that the patients are not inclined to pay their bill on time, if at all. It is also evident that the staff is not able to convey the value of the services rendered, and because of this shortcoming, the cash flow of the office is often compromised. Remember, expenses are a function of production, not collection.

A careful assessment of A/Rs should be made, including how much of the A/Rs is insurance. An annual review of how much is written off as a function of gross production will give you an idea of how healthy your receivables are.

It is recommended that an amount equal to approximately one month's production be maintained as accounts receivable. A greater amount than this creates a cash management issue and perhaps a cash flow issue. Less than this amount can suggest less-than-aggressive diagnosing and treatment planning-case acceptance and/or may allow for large fluctuations in monthly income due to productivity levels.

Remember, a buyer is going to look at the A/Rs as an indicator of practice health. If healthy, A/Rs can be sold to the buyer for very little discount. Insurance A/Rs are worth a dollar-for-dollar amount and internally financed contract A/Rs are usually discounted by as much as 40% of value depending on collectability.

CHARTING—Complete legible charts are critical to transference of patients in a transition. Obviously, accurate clinical notes and periodontal charting should be contained in the patient records. It is also important to include personal notes that include concerns and motivators of the patient as well as family issues and anything that will allow for an intimate reference that will enhance the dentist-patient relationship.

The charts should be well-organized with the information easy to find and interpret. As dental practices move toward electronic charting and paperless offices, it should become easier to maintain accurate, current clinical notes, but it is also important to keep track of patient histories and personal information.

It is estimated that for every $600,000 of production in a practice, there is $300,000 of treatment planned and accepted dentistry in the charts waiting to be completed. It is critical for potential buyers to do chart reviews or audits to determine what dentistry has been completed and how much dentistry is left in the existing patient base for the buyer to do. If all the dentistry has been done, as in the case of many cosmetic practices, the buyer may be purchasing a maintenance practice with little operative and restorative dentistry left to do.

INSURANCE—Reduced fee insurance is a pet peeve! In today's dental marketplace, reduced fee insurance is absolutely unnecessary in most dental markets. With fewer and fewer dentists available to treat more and more people, it is totally unnecessary to compromise your earnings by reducing the UCR fees established in your office. You are subsidizing the dental insurance industry.

There is some confusion about indemnity insurance versus Preferred Provider Organizations (PPOs) and Health Maintenance Organizations (HMOs). All are insurance industry products meant to make money for the insurance industry. Indemnity insurance is a product that is purchased by the consumer in order to pay for or offset the cost of dental procedures at no disadvantage or discount to the dentist. PPOs and HMOs, on the other hand, expect the dentist to pay part of the cost of the dentistry in the form of a discount to the patient. The patient, or more often, the employer of the patient, pays a smaller insurance premium for limited benefits as defined in the plan and expects the dentist to contribute anywhere from 10% to 30% of his or her fee to provide the dental service.

This insidious abuse of the health care industry by insurance companies began in the late seventies and early eighties when there was a competitive environment in dentistry. The insurance industry saw a crack in the dike and inserted themselves with the threat that dentists who did not participate would fail. Unfortunately, medicine caved in to the threat and all but a few elective procedures in medicine are insurance-controlled.

The following chart will show that a 20% reduction of UCR will cost 70% in net income, which places you in the position that you are making little more per hour than your dental hygienist.

Single Crown	100% UCR	80% UCR	70% UCR
Fee	$1,000	$800	$700
Preparation	1 hour	1 hour	1 hour
Cementation	.75 hour	.75 hour	.75 hour
TOTAL TIME	1.75 hour	1.75 hour	1.75 hour
Laboratory fee	$200	$200	$200
Supplies	$ 50	$ 50	$ 50
Fixed Expenses			
$200/hour X 1.75 hours	$350	$350	$350
PRE-TAX EARNINGS	$400	$200	$100
EARNINGS PER HOUR	$229	$114	$57

Some dentists suggest that they will hire an associate to do the reduced-fee dentistry and allow them to do the fee-for-service procedures. If the dentist pays the associate 35% of his collections, he is actually losing money.

Compensation for a $700 crown at 35% is $245. If the dentist's net income on this procedure is $57, he is losing $188 on every crown the associate performs on a patient with reduced-fee insurance.

The bottom line is that most buyers do not want to purchase a reduced-fee practice, and they are being advised in dental school of the pitfalls of reduced-fee dentistry.

STAFF—Needless to say, a well-trained staff is critical to any practice. A good team is critical to any transition and is the stabilizing factor when the new dentist takes over. Established staff members know the patients and can bridge the anxiety of patients with the new dentist.

An analysis of staff attrition, salaries, benefits, and training is necessary to determine the risk associated with buying a practice. Staff that is overpaid, undertrained, or underutilized compromises the net income of the practice, thus impacting the value of the practice. Staff that is constantly turning over suggests management problems in the practice, and reasons for the turnover should be investigated.

If staff members are overpaid or underpaid with salary and benefits, adjustments need to be made on the income and expense statement at the time of an appraisal to bring those expenses into line with the acceptable range norms. An office manager who is a spouse paid two or three times the going rate will have to be replaced with an office manager paid in line with his or her experience and duties. On the other hand, if an office manager who is a spouse is not paid, or is underpaid, a similar adjustment must be made to compensate a similar staff member. This addition will reflect on the bottom line of the income statement and most likely will affect the value of the practice.

A schedule of salaries, benefits, hours, tenure, and skill levels will provide a buyer and an appraiser with a clear picture of the value or risk the staff is to a practice. Of all the systems, a well-trained, well-established team can be the greatest asset of the practice.

FACILITY—Though rarely thought of as a system, it is included here because it is important when doing an appraisal of the practice. For a practice sale to be financed by a lender, the purchaser of the practice has to be able to secure a lease for at least the term of the loan, or they must be able to purchase the real estate. Lenders also do not want to lend money for a transition if the facility has to have major upgrades or is not functional to the point of providing the environment in which the buyer of the practice can generate adequate income to meet his or her financial obligations.

It is not critical that the equipment be brand new and state of the art, but it is important that it is in good working condition, looks decent, and allows the buyer to perform dentistry in a satisfactory manner.

It doesn't work to have a right-handed dentist buy a practice that is built out for a left-handed dentist. Most buyers expect the basic equipment in an office to be reasonably modern, including good hand pieces, sharp instruments, fiber optics, and up-to-date computer hardware and software.

However, it is very important to reiterate that equipment is the least important asset in the appraisal or purchase. Equipment can be inexpensively replaced compared to the overall value of the office and the goodwill associated with it.

It is not difficult to evaluate a lot about a practice just by looking at the facility. Is it clean? Is it neat? Is the equipment well maintained (regardless of age)? Are the furnishings relatively modern and comfortable, or is there brown shag carpet and plastic chairs in the reception area? Is the office OSHA compliant?

Remember, first impressions are lasting impressions. A potential buyer will be either impressed or disappointed with what the office looks like.

RECALL—The hygiene department is the heart of a practice! If the practice has a weak hygiene department, it is a weak practice. Hygiene should account for approximately 23% of the practice gross revenue, and there should be one hygiene day per week for every 200 active patients. Active patients are defined as *any* patient seen in the previous eighteen months. This includes one-time-only patients, regular hygiene patients, and operative/restorative patients. Different software programs generate different patient activity reports, and the adage "garbage in-garbage out" is true. It is not a bad idea to purge patient charts once a year, and in so doing, do a manual count of the active patients in a practice. This is very important to a buyer and is critical in analyzing a practice as an appraiser.

The hygienist should be a participating member of the office team as he or she should be identifying the patients' dental condition and preparing the patient for the diagnosis that the dentist may provide. The team relationship between the hygienist and the dentist is critical for each practitioner in establishing confidence in the other. A competent, engaged hygienist will generate significant dentistry from his or her department.

If the hygiene revenue is significantly less than 23% of gross production, the patient recall system is probably not working. If there is more than one cancellation per day that is not filled or there are more than three no-shows a week, the system is broken.

On the other hand, if the hygiene department is generating significantly more than 23% of gross production, there may be a maintenance practice or that a problem with case-presentation or case-acceptance verbal skills.

These issues create risk in a practice, which lowers the value.

NEW PATIENTS—Where hygiene is the heart of a practice, new patients are the life blood. There should never be a situation where a practice stops taking new patients! Nor should there be a practice that is seeing sixty new patients a month. These situations suggest serious problems in a practice that are red flags of risk. When no new patients are being seen, the practice is dying, and when too many new patients are being seen, there is no way they can all be treated properly and on a regular basis.

The optimum for an established practice is for the practice to see one new patient per dentist per day. So for a four-day week, there would be four new patients a week or sixteen per month. These new patients should be included in the block scheduling so that the dentist can spend significant time examining the patient and developing a dentist/patient relationship. Dentistry is relationships. It is these relationships that will allow the treatment plans to be accepted.

The practice should have an ideal patient profile (in writing). Who is the ideal patient? How old? What economic status? What demographic profile? This ideal patient should, and most likely will, come from internal referrals of like patients. The practice should also keep track of new patients to ensure they are fitting the ideal profile. This is not to say that other patients would be turned away from the office, but, rather, as a suggestion of the type of patient they should be targeting to ask for visits and referrals from.

You should know the expected annual treatment revenue generated by your average new patient. This information should be tracked and analyzed with every new patient having the proposed treatment recorded. Periodically, the total treatment revenue should be divided by the total number of patients seen to provide an average new patient treatment value. It should be determined if this new treatment value meets the goals that have been set for the practice.

Another measure that should be analyzed is the ratio of treatment acceptance to treatment presented. The easiest way to get 100% case acceptance is to underdiagnose! With new patients, all treatment should be diagnosed and treatment planned for the patient. It cannot be expected that all of the patients will accept all of the treatment, but unless it is known what the percentage of acceptance is, it is impossible to evaluate the success of case presentation. If acceptance is low, it may indicate verbal skills issues or team support issues in the practice.

MARKETING—Marketing is an important system that requires a plan. Advertising is a form of marketing, but marketing goes well beyond advertising. Marketing includes propagating an image, developing a brand, and establishing and maintaining a reputation. It is easy to assume that the only marketing need is a Yellow Pages ad and easy to fall into the trap of a good salesperson selling a full-page advertisement or 1-800-DENTIST.

The first step in establishing a marketing plan is to determine what is needed. If there is a need for new patients, some kind of advertising may be indicated. If there are plenty of patients, but they don't fit the ideal patient profile that has been established, then advertising may not be the solution to the problem. It may be that an internal marketing plan is required to attract the right patients.

Marketing is a subspecialty in business schools and carries its own degree designation. Marketing professionals specialize in identifying markets and market profiles and targeting them. If money is going to be spent on marketing, it would be wise to consult with specialists who understand and have been successful in dental practice marketing. Marketing for a supermarket or clothing store is very different than marketing for a dental practice, and the learning curve to educate a non-dental-oriented marketing person to understand what dentistry is, what your ideal patient profile consists of, and how to attract that patient to your practice may cost more than it produces.

It is important to note that it is not always necessary or advisable to select a corporate or operational name that is not your own. The idea that a practice named solely after the owner is harder to transition than that of a corporate name is a fallacy. Branding does not relate to a nonpersonalized corporate name; it is perfectly acceptable and certainly plausible to brand a personal DDS/DMD, PA, or the like.

With the future changes in the demographics in dentistry and with the ratio of dentists to patients decreasing dramatically, it may be very prudent to carefully evaluate the need to market at all, except internally. Very rarely do advertising, coupons, mailings, and so forth attract the ideal patient.

Entire books and textbooks have been written about

marketing and business development. Suffice it to say that two or three paragraphs on the subject are inadequate to inform and advise, other than to indicate a need to seek out those with knowledge and expertise in the field.

Seller's Issues and Concerns

The sale of your dental practice is a big decision that should not be made lightly. There are different reasons for dentists to consider selling, the most common of which is retirement. Other reasons may be relocation, disability, specialization, or for other personal reasons.

Whatever the reason, the first step is to be sure that you have made the decision for the right reasons and are comfortable with that decision. Often, dentists sell their practice thinking they are ready to give up the hand piece, only to realize that they miss the dentistry, the patients, and being a doctor, or they just get bored and want to go back to practicing again.

The biggest miscalculation is economic. Retirement planning is critical when making the decision to retire from practice. The amount of money that will be received from the sale of the practice is not going to meet your retirement needs. So the first step in making the retirement decision is to have a certified financial planner prepare a financial plan that provides the information of what the financial needs and projections are for your specific lifestyle.

There are different services that financial planners offer. It is important to find a financial planner who is interested in providing you with information, not selling you management services. If money management services are what you are looking for, you can find them in many places once you have a financial plan in place. It is okay to use a financial planner who provides management services, but many are interested in getting your money into their account, because that is where they make their big money. The costs of a financial plan are very reasonable relative to the information and planning that is provided.

As part of your financial planning, the value of your practice has to be considered along with all of your other assets. This requires that you have an appraisal of the practice done and have it regularly updated, because the value may change due to practice or market issues.

Once you are comfortable with your retirement planning, you should optimize the practice so that it sells for the highest value. The biggest contributor to increased value is, again, increasing the net income. That means improving systems, lowering overhead, and not letting the practice gross income decline.

One big mistake sellers make is excessive capital expenditures with the idea that a new, high-tech office will sell better than the existing practice. As has been stated here before, equipment is the least valuable element of the practice value, and major capital expenditures take up to seven years to recover. Furthermore, the buyer of the practice may have his or her own ideas about what equipment they want to use or replace.

This is not to say that cosmetic improvements should not be done. Replacing worn carpet, painting walls, and updating technology are all expenses that can make a significant difference in the saleability of a practice. But the most important and most valuable asset of the practice is the goodwill, the patients, the dental team, and the functionality of the practice.

Other considerations that should be made when contemplating the sale of the practice are:

- Are staff members going to stay with the buyer, or are they going to retire?

- Is employee compensation appropriate for the market place?

- Is the lease assignable or renewable to accommodate the buyer?

- Is all of the equipment functioning properly?

- If the practice is referral-based, will the referrers continue to send patients?

- How are existing accounts receivable going to be handled after the transfer?

As you review these preparatory steps, other questions and concerns are likely to arise and should be considered as you approach retirement.

It is also important to contemplate who your advisors and consultants are going to be. Certainly your attorney, financial planner, and accountant should be considered. Are you going to try to sell the practice on your own, or are you going to use a broker? If so, whom and why?

Some of the considerations in selecting a broker are:

- How long has the broker been working with dental practice sales?

- What is the broker's experience in my local market?

- What services does the broker provide?

- Will the broker work with my attorney and my accountant?

- Does the broker represent me, or does he represent the buyer as well (dual representation)?

- What is the broker's reputation for successful transactions?

- What kind of exposure (marketing) does the broker provide?

- What lending institutions recommend and work with the broker?

- What is the term of the listing agreement, and can I terminate it without penalties?

- What is the commission and/or other fees that I will be paying to the broker?

Again, these are some of the questions that should be asked of a broker before agreeing to sign a listing agreement. Like every profession, there are very good brokers, mediocre brokers, and very poor brokers. Some brokers will tell the client whatever they want to hear to get the listing agreement, knowing full well that the market will ultimately determine the sale price of the practice to be significantly less than the seller's expectation.

It is also important to know that buyers inquire of all

the brokers for practice opportunities, not just one. Therefore, your practice will be ultimately exposed to potential buyers. Who do you want representing your interests when the right buyer comes along?

If you choose the wrong broker, and your practice is shopped to buyers, very often, even after changing brokers and arriving at a realistic value for the practice, the damage has been done in the buyer community.

Attorneys and accountants can also be either extremely helpful or a massive problem in consummating a transaction. There are attorneys and accountants who are very familiar with dental practice sales and those who are not. There are certain legal and tax provisions that are unique to dental practice transactions due to state and federal statutes and tax laws. The State Dental Act also has requirements that may have to be met when transferring patient records and selling goodwill and tangible assets. A good local broker will not only understand the legal and tax issues, but will be able to refer you to knowledgeable professionals who also understand the laws and tax implications.

Selling your practice for whatever reason is a very serious business, and finding the right professionals should be considered very carefully, not only for monetary reasons, but for peace of mind and to preserve your reputation as a servant in the community.

Buyer's Issues and Concerns

There are technically three categories of buyers: new dentists (just graduated), dentists who have worked as associates and are first-time buyers, and previous owner dentists who are relocating or merging.

There is a small percentage of dentists just out of school who decide they are interested in, capable of, and willing to purchase a dental practice. Some of the obvious issues that this dentist faces are:

- Clinical experience and speed

- Business management skills

- Personnel management skills

- Patient rapport skills

Some dentists out of school have acquired some of these skills and experience, but rarely do we see all of them mastered by a new dentist.

One of the major obstacles that a new dentist buyer faces is getting the financing to purchase a practice from the established lenders without practice experience. Most lenders require at least one, and usually two, years in a general practice residency or actual practice experience as an associate.

The other issue for many new dentists is they are not really settled into their life. In other words, they may not know in which location they want to settle down. There may be a marriage or children to consider in establishing in a location prematurely. The decision to buy a practice is a long-term commitment, much longer than buying a house, and should be very carefully evaluated and thought through. Working in an area as an associate for a year or two will provide the information about the people, the place, and the dental community that is necessary to have in making an informed decision.

Deciding to want to practice in Florida or California is not adequate. Pensacola is very different than Miami or Naples, and Los Angeles is so diverse that there are complete demographic societies that make up the neighborhoods. The economics of one place can be totally different from a community three miles away. Buying your first practice should take time and investigation to make sure you make the right choice.

The associate buyer is the most common. An associate has worked in one or more environments, developed clinical skills and speed, learned some management skills, and has decided on a location from experience in or with that area.

Often, associates are offered opportunities to buy into a practice as a partner, which we will discuss later, but many have decided that they are ready to own and manage their own practice and start the search.

The experienced dentist who has owned a practice and

has decided to relocate for one reason or another usually knows what he or she wants and has the experience and financial wherewithal to purchase a practice. He or she is usually looking for a very specific practice or practice location.

The experienced dentist is most often looking for the large, well-established practice that has a stable staff and strong patient base, practicing the kind of dentistry that they are comfortable practicing. There are some, though, who may relocate for a smaller retirement office, whereby they can cut the number of days per week they work from their previous practice and enjoy more personal time. While they may be looking for a smaller office in either physical or production size, they usually will be coming from a well-run, strong office and will look closely at the systems of an office prior to purchasing.

As different as all of these buyers are, there are common issues that each should be aware of and carefully examine as part of the due diligence that is performed in assessing the potential practice. A Buyer's Checklist is included in the appendix as a guideline to assist in making sure all the bases have been covered.

Buyers should never sign any commitment to a single broker and should not pay for the services of a broker unless the buyer is hiring the broker as the buyer's agent to represent the buyer in the transaction. Unlike the housing and commercial real estate industry, there is no multi-listing relationship between dental practice brokers. Therefore, they usually do not work together in selling each other's listings. It is imperative that, as a buyer, you keep your options open and watch all the listings that become available for purchase.

If you find a practice that you are interested in, but do not want to work with that particular broker, you can always hire a broker who you want to work with to represent you for a negotiated fee. If your broker is working on your behalf, it is likely you will save significant money, more than the fee paid, to have someone in your corner, looking out for your interests.

Careful analysis of the economics of the practice should be made with the help of someone who knows dental practice expenses as they relate to the practice income. This will expose any financial anomalies that may exist and will provide you with a reasonable projection of the income you can expect to make in the practice. This analysis should include examination of the practice income and expense statement and tax returns, including the expense schedules.

It is recommended that an equipment supply and/or repair person be allowed to examine the equipment to determine working order. Supplies should be examined, not just for quantity, but for type and currency. Are the medicaments current? What products are being used in the office? Computer software and hardware should be evaluated, and the condition and appearance of the office observed.

The patient charts should be reviewed to determine how many active charts (patients seen within the previous eighteen months) there are, and what kind and how much dentistry the patients are accepting. What referral sources, if any, provide patients to the practice?

Staff compensation and benefits should be evaluated along with the job descriptions and duties of team members.

This is just a partial list of information that should be gathered and evaluated by the buyer. If an appraisal has been done by a reputable appraiser, most of this information will already have been gathered and should be available in the appraisal report. Good practice software will generate reports that will provide most of the information required.

Evaluating this information constitutes the buyer's due diligence, which, when referred back to our fair market value definition, provides the reasonable knowledge for the buyer.

Associateships, Partnerships, and Practice Structure

An ongoing and ever-present interest in multi-practitioner relationships is inherent in dentistry, and there are many reasons dentists consider affiliating with one or more dentists. Most often, however, the reasons have not been thought through, the impact on the practice and team has not been analyzed, and, if a multi-dentist relationship is decided upon, the appropriate time and effort has not gone into the selection of a partner.

The most common shortcoming is the failure to properly understand and evaluate the economics of bringing in an associate or partner.

One hundred percent of multi-dentist relationships end! Some end in death or disability, some end in retirement, some end with philosophical or clinical differences, and some end for monetary reasons, but they all end.

To understand the risks and rewards of a multi-dentist relationship, we must understand the practice structure. The legal structure of a practice has significant liability and tax implications and should be evaluated and set up properly.

SOLE PROPRIETOR—A sole proprietor practice is one that is not incorporated (C Corporation or Subchapter S Corporation), does not have shared ownership, has not formed a Limited Liability Company (LLC), or a Limited Liability Partnership (LLP).

For many years, dentists and other professionals incorporated to provide personal liability protections and advanced retirement options not available to the sole proprietor. Malpractice insurance provides, in most cases, adequate liability coverage in dentistry, and a variety of retirement options is available within or without the corporate structure. The sole proprietor practice is an adequate structure for the solo dentist, and with exit strategy planning (retirement planning) with qualified financial planners, retirement plan options within the sole proprietor practice are available.

The sole proprietorship requires fewer tax forms to complete, less paperwork for state record keeping, and no fees to pay to maintain the practice structure.

LIMITED LIABILITY COMPANIES—A solo practice dentist can also practice as a Limited Liability Company (LLC). LLCs were created to avoid the red tape and corporate requirements that the government and states established for corporations. The LLCs are regulated by the state, but can elect either C Corporation or Subchapter S Corporation tax treatment by the Internal Revenue Service. LLCs provide the same corporate barrier between potential liability and the dentist personally.

LIMITED LIABILITY PARTNERSHIPS – Limited Liability Partnerships (LLP) are similar to LLCs. Most states have provisions for LLCs or LLPs, but not both. Both entities have the same liability protection function and both have C Corporation or Subchapter S Corporation tax election.

There is now adequate case law with regard to the liability protections of LLCs and LLPs, and most are considered to provide a firewall between any liability created by the practice and the dentist's personal assets. It must be stated here, however, that in the event of a serious infraction that points back to personal negligence, the dentist, most likely, will be sued and face some personal liability, regardless of corporate structure.

Owners of LLCs or LLPs are designated as members. Usually, there is a managing member designated, denoting the person responsible for administrating the LLC or LLP. The legal document governing the LLC or LLP is an operating agreement. This agreement serves to provide the structure and organization of the LLP or LLC.

SCHEDULE C CORPORATION—A Schedule C Corporation was the structure of choice prior to the 1986 tax law changes. It provided liability protection for the dentist(s) and offered retirement planning benefits that were not available to the sole proprietor. A Schedule C Corporation often includes "Inc." or "Incorporated" in the legal name of the practice. As a corporation, the dentist is usually the president and secretary of the corporation, and in most states, the only officer and shareholder due to the fact that it is not legal for a nondentist (including a spouse) to own an equity interest in a dental practice unless a licensed dentist in that state. (Consult your State Dental Practice Act.) All parties in a C Corporation are shareholders, and they own stock in the corporation.

A corporation is a legal entity. This means that the corporation is an autonomous entity. Consider the corporation as another "person." The corporation can own assets, can have liabilities, and can pay taxes. Any profit retained by the corporation is taxed by the government and by many states. Once the corporate profit has been taxed, the remaining profit is passed through to the shareholders (the dentist) and is taxed a second time. This can be a disadvantage to having a dental practice as a C Corporation. Taxes and tax issues will be discussed in a separate chapter, but a seller must be advised that there can be very significant tax consequences when it comes to selling a practice that is incorporated as a C Corporation.

SUBCHAPTER S CORPORATION – A Subchapter S Corporation (S Corp) under the Internal Revenue Code is also a corporation, but allows for the profits of the corporation to be passed through to the shareholder (dentist) without being taxed at the corporate level. Obviously, the dentist will pay taxes on the income generated by the corporation, but it is single taxation, not double taxation as in the C Corporation. This also applies to the sale of the assets owned by the Subchapter S Corporation when they are sold. The proceeds of the sale will pass through to the dentist and be taxed only once.

As with the C Corporation, the dentist owner is usually the president and secretary and the only shareholder in the Subchapter S Corporation. Most Subchapter S Corporations are designated as PAs, or PCs. All dentist owners, if more than one, are shareholders and own stock in the corporation.

In the corporate structure, Subchapter S or C Corporation, corporate bylaws and a shareholder agreement govern and regulate the activities of the corporation and the stockholders.

PARTNERSHIPS—True partnerships are potentially one of the riskiest entities in which to be a party. Partnerships expose every party to liability for every other party in a true partnership, without respect to ownership percentage, even if no liability was incurred as a matter of the business enterprise. The liabilities incurred by one partner can, and most often do, become the liabilities of the other partner(s).

Even though a relationship is often referred to as a partnership, most relationships are formed in the context of a corporation (C or Subchapter S), an LLC, or an LLP, and these entities do not share the same liabilities between the parties as a true partnership.

When two parties work together; share a common business name and perform the same, similar, or supporting activities; and share common responsibilities, the relationship can be viewed and treated as an ostensible partnership, and the liabilities will most often be shared by each party.

Partnerships are easy to enter into and often just evolve as two parties begin to work together. However, this evolution without consideration for the unwinding of the relationship and without the proper documents that define the relationship, especially the dissolution provisions, can, and usually does, become a nightmare when trying to end the relationship.

If entering into a partnership, comprehensive indemnification language should be a part of the partnership agreement. Indemnification language only provides that the committing party will protect the other party(s) from liability. It does not assure that the other party(s) will not be included in litigation or ultimately be held liable or partially liable in a lawsuit. Unfortunately, we are a litigious society, and those with deep pockets are invariably named as defendants in lawsuits, even if they have no actual participation or liability.

Now that we have defined the different entity structures available to the dental practice, the question is, "Which one is best for my practice?" and if considering a transition, "How does my present entity impact that transition?"

THE MULTI-DENTIST PRACTICE—There are many reasons to consider entering into a multi-dentist relationship. Some are valid; some are not. As stated before, the biggest mistakes in entering into a multi-dentist relationship are doing so for the wrong reason, not taking the time to find the right relationship, and not understanding the economics. See Graph #4

Some of the reasons for a dentist to bring on an associate are to reduce busyness, improve the senior doctor's lifestyle, function as the senior doctor's exit strategy, increase procedure mix, and encourage practice growth. If one or more of these reasons does not exist, it is unlikely that an associate is going to be in the best interest of the practice.

Some of the wrong reasons to bring on an associate are to utilize the facility more, reduce the chaos that exists because of poor management, allow for more comprehensive procedures by senior dentists, or to pass reduced fee

Graph 4

Private Dental Practices by Size (2005–2010)[1],[2],[3],(A),(B)

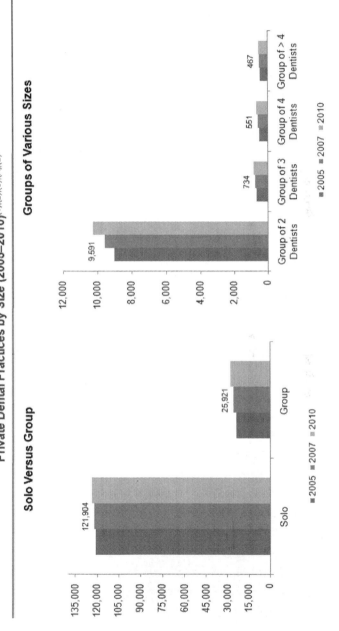

Solo Versus Group

Groups of Various Sizes

dentistry to the associate (preserving the fee-for-service dentistry for the senior doctor).

There are some basic rules of thumb that can be utilized to determine whether an associate can be accommodated.

Facility size has to be an initial consideration. In the optimal dental practice, each dentist should have at least two treatment rooms in order to allow for proper scheduling. There also needs to be an adequate number of treatment rooms for hygiene. Remember the hygiene formula: One hygiene day per week for every 200 active patients. To consider adding a full-time associate, the practice should have at least 2,000 active patients. Less patients than this will not be enough to keep two full time dentists busy. Two thousand active patients requires ten hygiene days per week, which means two full-time hygiene treatment rooms. To reiterate, active patients are unique patients who have been in within the last eighteen months; a report from your practice management software may be inaccurate. Any combination of consulting with an experienced transition specialist, a thorough chart audit, or the assistance of a practice management add-on software package, such as Sikka Software, will yield the accurate number.

Two treatment rooms per dentist and two for hygiene indicates a need for at least six treatment rooms required to bring an associate into the practice. In some cases, alternating schedules or having hyper-hygiene days (three or four treatment rooms for hygiene) can work for a while with less than six treatment rooms, but eventually, as the practice grows, which is the goal, the required number of treatment rooms to accommodate each dentist and the hygienists will be required.

With the above formulas, it will be relatively easy to project the facility requirements when considering whether to add an associate to the practice.

Busyness can be caused by at least two possibilities. As stated before in the systems discussion, if scheduling is not efficient, busyness will prevail. If reduced-fee managed care is a large part of the practice, busyness can be a problem because of too many patients getting free or reduced fee dentistry.

Hiring an associate to reduce busyness, in most cases, will not solve the problem and, in many cases, will exacerbate it. In addition, the associate will cost you out-of-pocket money if doing procedures that you would ordinarily be doing.

In a reduced-fee practice, the associate will be paid on collections, which means that if the UCR is reduced by 10% to 20%, and the associate is making the market 30% to 35% of collections, the practice will be actually losing money on most procedures the associate performs. (Refer back to the chart on page 39.) It is unlikely that you will be able to find an associate who is willing to work for less than a hygienist.

If the busyness problem is ineffective scheduling, hiring an associate will only complicate the scheduling process and compound the chaos in the office. Fixing the schedule and reducing or eliminating reduced fee dentistry will reduce the busyness and thus reduce the chaos.

If the associate is being hired to allow the owner dentist more time off, and if all the systems in the practice are functioning properly, an associate might very well accomplish this need. Obviously, adequate facility and hours of practice must be offered to make it a reasonable opportunity for the associate. Unless you can find a "worker bee" (someone who wants to just work and not become a partner) who is willing to work one or two days a week, or partial days, it is not likely that a part-time job for the associate is going to work for him or her. Most dentists, by nature, are entrepreneurs and are looking to own and to be in control. Unless this opportunity is available, a long-term relationship with an associate is unlikely. Therefore, it is the owner-dentist who will need to become the part-time dentist, and this will mean a cut in pay. If this is okay, and it is the goal to reduce time in the office, an associate may be the answer. However, once again, it is critical to evaluate the economics of the plan before putting it into place to determine if the financial results will be satisfactory to all concerned.

For a multi-dentist office to work, whether a full or part-time associate or for a partnership, the relationship has to be win-win if it is to last. Turnstile relationships will weaken and create lasting damage to a dental practice with patients and staff alike.

As an exit strategy, bringing an associate into the practice to buy in and ultimately buy out upon the retirement of the senior dentist is a very justifiable and usually successful reason to hire an associate. Once the goals have been set for retirement, the economics, including retirement planning, have been evaluated, and a decision has been made to begin a transition to retirement, the process of finding the right candidate can begin. A word of caution: *take your time!* The biggest mistake dentists make is bringing the associate into the practice without doing the required planning and economic analysis.

Once a potential candidate has been identified as a

possible successor, several steps should be taken to keep the process on track. A defined timetable should be established for the entire process, which should include a trial period, associate period, the buy-in, the-partnership period, and the buyout. There may potentially be a seller associateship period as well. All of these steps should be clearly defined in the beginning of the relationship and not haphazardly as the associateship progresses. Let's examine each one of these steps.

The trial period should be a six-month period of time with no obligations or requirements of either party. The only defined issues should be compensation and work responsibilities. There should be no restrictive covenant, and the employment should be "at will," meaning that either party can terminate the relationship for any reason. This should be a period of evaluation of personality, clinical skills, philosophy, and social skills. The dental team should be involved in assessing the associate's compatibility with the practice, the team, and the patients.

Once the trial period is complete, the associate should be offered an employment agreement, a legally binding contract that defines the associate's duties, responsibilities, and compensation and should include termination provisions and a restrictive covenant and/or a nonsolicitation agreement.

Prior to entering into the employment agreement and during the trial period, the associate should be given specific information about the buy-in time frame and estimated cost, including economic predictions of why and how it will be a successful partnership as well as the expectations for the buyout with anticipated time frame and cost. This information will keep the associate on a buy-in track and provide incentive for him or her to make the commitment to the practice.

The partnership period begins at the buy-in and is triggered by the economic analysis that supports the buy-in. All too often, a date is set for the buy-in, and both parties are surprised that the economics don't work out. Remember, that once the associate becomes a partner (assuming 50% ownership), he or she will be responsible for 50% of the overhead, will get credit for 50% of the hygiene revenue, and will have to pay the debt service for the buy-in. Unless these numbers are analyzed and understood, either or both parties may be surprised that the buy-in does not work. The partnership period may last several years, more or less, but there should be a defined buyout date agreed upon so both parties can plan accordingly. This date does not have to be in stone but should reflect the genuine intent of each of the partners.

The buyout should occur on or before a "date certain" that is defined in the shareholder agreement in the corporation or the operating agreement in an LLC or LLP. The buyout provisions should define what triggers a buyout (death, disability, voluntary retirement) and the process that takes place, particularly the financial arrangements, including the price paid for the remaining half of the practice, the method of paying for it, and any insurance provisions that will be utilized in the event of death or disability, including who the owners of the policies are and who the beneficiaries are.

Often, the selling partner decides to stay on as an associate to the buyer for a period of time after the buyout. If this is agreed to, the seller should have an employment agreement with the same provisions, terms, and conditions as the buyer had as an associate in the practice. "What is good for the goose is good for the gander." In setting up this process as a potential seller, it should be kept in mind that the table could turn and the terms and conditions that are offered to the associate-buyer may be the same terms and conditions that will be offered after the buyout.

Once again, a word of caution. There are some companies that are setting up exit strategy transitions that are very one-sided in that they are building a retirement fund on the back of an associate by suggesting very low compensation for a period of time, with an escrowed fund that will apply to the buyout and a fixed buyout price set at the beginning of the relationship. Very few of these relationships actually succeed for several reasons. The associate is not making enough money to survive the buy-in period and usually finds a better opportunity and moves on. In so doing, the associate loses the escrowed money to the seller, which does not make for good feelings. Also, very often the value of the practice increases over the period of time the associate is in the practice, and often the seller is not happy about selling the practice at such a low value. If, in fact, this process is undertaken and the associate leaves, it creates chaos in the practice, and the exit strategy process has to start again.

Once again, evaluation of the economics of the transaction should be carefully analyzed, and the terms and conditions should be reviewed by knowledgeable counselors and advisors.

Transition Options

The following are transition options that are most common:

- Sell the practice outright
- Sell a percentage of the practice
  - As a sole proprietor
    - Form a partnership
    - Form a corporation (Subchapter S, recommended)
    - Establish an LLC or LLP
  - As a corporation (S or C)
    - Sell stock (only option for partnership)
  - As an LLC or LLP
    - Must sell membership interest
- Mergers
- Close the practice and walk away

SELL THE PRACTICE—Selling the practice outright is the most successful, least risky, and least encumbering process of transition. The seller walks away with cash in hand and does not have to look back or be responsible for any multi-doctor issues.

Usually, the selling dentist has reached a retirement point and is moving on to another phase in life. The purchaser is going to take the seller's practice and create his or her own practice by building on the foundation that was laid by the seller.

To accomplish a successful win-win sale, the first step is to determine a fair selling price for the practice. Usually, this involves bringing in an expert who has the required information, knowledge, and experience to properly value the practice.

It is not uncommon for the seller to think that the practice is worth more than it actually is. A lot of personal effort has gone into making the practice what it is, including the reputation that has taken years to develop and the relationships with patients that are very personal and important to the dentist. Nonetheless, the value is the price someone is willing to pay for the practice, and that is usually determined by the marketplace. An appropriate and valid appraisal will define what that marketplace is and assure that the value arrived at cash flows for potential buyers. Remember, the buyer has got to pay the overhead of the practice, the debt service (the loan to purchase the practice), and take a reasonable personal salary. If the practice is priced too high, it will not cash flow, and no one will be able or willing to buy it. Beware of brokers who are willing to list your practice for sale at an unrealistic high price in order to get the listing. The bottom line is that the practice will sell for market value! That means that your expectations will ultimately not be met if the value is set unreasonably high.

It is not only the buyers who will balk at the high price, but the lenders as well, who know what the market is. They do very detailed cash flow analyses and will not lend if the numbers do not work. So even if a naïve buyer can be talked into an unrealistic purchase price, reputable lenders will not lend the money. At some point, buyers will cease to be interested in the practice, even if and when the price is lowered to within the market range. Practices that have been shopped this way cause a red flag with buyers because they are looking for something wrong with the practice that has caused other potential buyers to reject it.

On the other hand, it is not uncommon for a buyer to want to pay less than the asking price, even if it is set at a legitimate market value.

One of the concerns a buyer uses to negotiate a lower price is patient attrition. Nationally, it has been determined than only 2%–3% of patients leave a practice when it changes hands. Most patients will remain in the practice long enough for the new dentist to meet them and provide some initial treatment. If the new dentist is too aggressive, has an unpleasant personality, is rough, and/or causes pain or discomfort for the patient, it is likely the attrition rate will be higher.

Once a tentative agreement has been reached, a transition strategy should be developed by the buyer and the seller in order to notify staff and patients of the pending practice sale. Once the process has gone this far, the rumor mill has already started spreading the word. It won't be long until people will be asking questions, so it is important to be proactive in order to create a positive transition environment. It is natural for people to resist change, especially when it is unknown change. By bringing the team into the loop, you can control the information that is circulated and make it positive for the practice and the transaction.

Usually, a letter from the selling dentist to the patients of record, announcing his or her plans to retire and providing supportive and useful information about the buyer, is very helpful in letting the patients know what to expect on their next dental visit. The letter *should not* be sent out until all the legal documents are signed, the financing has been secured and the transaction has closed. As Yogi Berra said, "It ain't over 'til it's over!" The deal is not a deal until the ink has dried, and the money has changed hands. It is very embarrassing and damaging to send out letters announcing retirement and introducing the new doctor, only to have the deal fall through.

The ideal transition includes a minimal amount of time for the selling dentist to finish up cases that have been started, introduce the buyer to the staff and the systems used in the office, show where the light and vacuum switches are, and review what suppliers and labs are used. This should be accomplished in two or three weeks. If the seller has established relationships with patients, as would be expected, and the seller remains in the office, it can be expected that those patients will want their work performed by the seller. If the right value has been placed on the practice, the buyer will not be able to afford to have the seller doing all the dentistry. The seller cannot expect to sell the practice, stay as an associate, and make all the money. It is what my good friend Roger Hill calls "selling the cow and keeping the milk!"

SELLING A PERCENTAGE OF THE PRACTICE—Selling a percentage of the practice can occur regardless of the legal structure you have engaged in. There are very different tax treatments for different types of sales, so it is imperative that careful consideration be given to this process. We will discuss the tax treatment of each type of sale and its consequences to the seller and the buyer in a later chapter.

If you are a corporation (C or Subchapter S) you will need to sell stock in the corporation to the buyer. If you sell stock, you will receive very beneficial capital gains tax treatment; however, the buyer will not be able to write off or amortize the amount of money paid for the stock, nor will he or she be able to write off the interest for the loan taken to purchase the stock because the loan was to purchase a security (the stock is a security). In other words, it is very disadvantageous for the buyer to purchase the stock in a dental practice, and most attorneys or financial consultants would discourage a purchaser from doing so. We will discuss the options to create a win-win sale and purchase later.

If you are a sole proprietor, you can sell an interest in the practice assets, which include the tangible and intangible (goodwill) assets without the tax disadvantages of the corporate sale environment. Tax wise, the tangible assets value will be treated as ordinary income, and the goodwill will be treated as a capital gain for the seller. The buyer can write off 100% of the purchase price. This creates a win-

win environment for the transaction, but what is created in this transaction is a partnership, official or ostensible. Therefore, it is suggested that at the time of the sale, an entity such as a corporation, LLC, or LLP be created.

The corporation, LLC, or LLP can perform the function of providing the liability barrier and provides limited indemnification for each of the parties by any other party. If a true partnership is formed, it will not preclude the possibility of individual liability of each or the partners by or from the other partner(s). It is for this personal liability protection that the corporate or LLC/LLP structure is highly recommended in multi-doctor practices.

Once a total purchase price has been agreed upon by the parties, that purchase price has to be broken down into what is being purchased and for how much. This breakdown of the purchase price is known as allocating the purchase price, or the allocations. Usually, these allocations include equipment, supplies, goodwill, and, sometimes, restrictive covenant or other line items. The value that is placed on each of the items allocated needs to be agreed upon by the parties because each person, buyer and seller, has to file an IRS Form 8594 which identifies the allocations of the sale. Both forms, buyer's and seller's, have to have the same amounts allocated.

The amounts allocated for each item is arbitrary (as long as it is reasonable) and can be massaged to afford the best tax treatment for each of the parties. Because the allocations each have different tax consequences for both the buyer and seller, it is important to consult with someone familiar with the tax implications to make sure that the allocations are made in the most optimum way for both buyer and seller. It is why, at this point, it is critical to include the accountant in the discussions because only he or she knows the personal tax issues of their client. With the proper allocations agreed upon, again, a win-win relationship can be arrived at.

MERGERS—Mergers are a very successful and profitable transition model. However, they are one of the most difficult for several reasons. First, the practices have to be within a certain geographic proximity in order for the patients to migrate to a new location. The distance usually depends on the size of the city. If residents are used to traveling throughout the community for all their needs and services, it really won't matter where in the community the practices are located; however, if they have to travel outside their normal community boundaries, there will be attrition.

Other issues are the duplication of equipment, the dentist's philosophy, and most difficult, duplication of staff. It will most likely be necessary to eliminate some staff members, which can be very challenging.

Usually, the most difficult issue to resolve is the facilities. One of them has to be eliminated and, unless the lease is up, it can be hard to sublease the vacant office space. Therefore, timing is very important if considering a merger.

Nonetheless, mergers are the most expedient way to instantly increase the production in a dental practice, and, if properly handled, can be extremely successful.

CLOSE THE PRACTICE AND WALK AWAY—This certainly does not seem to be the optimum transition process! However, the realities facing dentistry for the foreseeable future should be re-examined. As was stated earlier, there is now and will continue to be a shortage of dentists, especially the specialties required to meet the public need. This will create more and more of a buyers' market because there will be more sellers than available buyers. There will also be more opportunity to start from scratch, eliminating the need to buy an existing practice. This will never, however, eliminate the optimum practice that has all its systems in order and has a high net income from being a very marketable practice. To meet the optimum standard, this practice must have relatively new equipment, current technology, up-to-date clinical methodology, and well-trained employees. It also needs to be located where the local demographic wants, needs, and willingness to pay for the best dental care available exist.

Assuming this is not your plan, your transition plan will be to bring in an associate several years before you retire and ultimately sell him or her your practice. Before you proceed, it is critical that you examine and understand the economics of this type of transition.

When you bring on an associate, you will be giving up a portion of the production that you would normally perform. You will have to pay the associate the going percentage rate while still having the same or greater overhead. In the process, you will give up a certain amount of net income until the associate is producing independently of you. This usually takes from one and a half to three years. It is also a fact that the average practice employs two or three associates before the right one is identified. With a five-year exit strategy, the risk is not worth the reward.

If your practice remains approximately the same size, and the associate assumes 20% of your production each year for the five years of the transition, then five years times 20% = 100%! Had you just maximized your production for those five years, you would have made the same amount you gave up to the associate, and you could then sell the practice for whatever or just walk away with the same amount of money (plus the purchase price).

This scenario was played out a few years ago when the practice management companies were offering to buy everyone's practice for one times gross. They would offer a small down payment and stock (that never appreciated), and require a 20% reduction in the seller's pay for a five-year employment contract to offset the management responsibilities that they were going to take over. Five years at a 20% reduction in pay provided that the seller actually bought his own practice back over the five-year period of time.

It must be emphasized that it is critically important for a selling dentist to develop a clear and defined exit strategy and to understand the economic consequences of the decisions that are made. It is not uncommon for dentists in the twilight of their years in practice to make a mistake that severely impacts their ability to retire comfortably or that impacts the value of the practice itself.

Another big problem that is seen is the dentist who is approaching retirement and begins to slow down and/or starts to "watch" treatment. Buyers are always looking at the production trends, and when a buyer sees a practice that is trending towards lower gross production, it raises a red flag that is interpreted as a dying practice. This is not necessarily the case, and in fact, it can be argued that there is more dentistry for the buyer to do, but that is not the interpretation that the buyer makes. The buyer will automatically begin to negotiate on the asking price because of the declining numbers. Buyers look for any reason to adjust the asking price downward, and the two biggest arguments are old equipment and declining production.

Tax Implications

In previous chapters, some of the tax issues relating to selling or buying all or part of a dental practice were mentioned. This is one of the most critical areas of concern in a transition and can be a very costly one if not done with forethought and the use of knowledgeable advisors. It is possible that a seller could give up as much as 60%–70% of the sale proceeds to taxes if the sale is not structured properly—and it does happen. It must be remembered that many attorneys and accountants have never been involved in the sale or transition of a dental practice. Therefore, you need advisors who understand and are aware of current tax rulings and how they impact you as a buyer or seller.

Earlier, we discussed allocations, the way the individual assets were valued as part of the sale. The only reason these allocations are made is for tax purposes because of the different amount of taxes paid for different assets by the seller and different depreciation or amortization (write-offs) schedules for the buyer.

Before the 1986 tax law changes, buyers and sellers were on opposing sides of the field when it came to how much to allocate to the different assets. What was advantageous to the seller was detrimental to the buyer and vice versa. Fortunately today, the tax environment allows that both the buyer and seller can have beneficial tax treatment if the assets are properly allocated.

Remember, the ordinary income tax bracket for most sellers, and for that matter, for most buyers is presently 35%, which means that for every dollar received as ordinary income, thirty-five cents will be paid in taxes. The current capital gains tax rate is 15%; therefore, for every dollar received as a capital gain, fifteen cents is paid in taxes. Therefore, it is desirable for the seller to allocate as much to capital gains as possible.

For the buyer, all of the assets can be depreciated or amortized (written off) over varying periods of time. It is important for the buyer to have a tax strategy before determining how to allocate in order to take full advantage of these depreciable assets.

The following chart breaks down the tax treatment for each of the assets usually allocated in a practice sale for each, the seller and the buyer.

Asset	Seller	Buyer
Accounts Receivables	Ordinary Income	Collected Tax Free
Supplies / Instruments	Ordinary Income	Expensed
Equipment	Recapture Depreciation + Capital Gains	Depreciated over five to seven years
Patient Records	Capital Gain	Amortized over 15 years
Goodwill	Capital Gain	Amortized over 15 years
Consulting Agreement	Ordinary Income + Payroll Taxes	Deductable as Paid
Deferred Compensation	Ordinary Income + Payroll Taxes	Deductable as Paid
Restrictive Covenant	Ordinary Income	Amortized over 15 years
Stock	Capital Gain	Nondeductable
Leasehold Improvements	Ordinary Income	Depreciated over 39.5 years

Examining each of these asset allocations will give both buyer and seller a better understanding of how important the allocation process is when buying or selling a dental practice.

ACCOUNTS RECEIVABLE—Accounts receivable can be, and often are, sold by the seller and purchased by the buyer. The money received is the same as if receiving fees for dentistry performed; therefore, they are treated for the seller as ordinary income. Since the taxes will have been paid by the seller, the buyer will collect them up to the amount paid and will not have to pay taxes on them. If, however, the buyer purchases the accounts receivable at a discount—which is normal—then any amount collected over what was paid for the receivables will be taxed as ordinary income. It is important for the buyer to make a note of this for his or her tax preparation, which may be a year away, so that if paid accounts receivable are being collected along with the normal fees during the year, the accounts receivable are separated out from the regular fees in order to not pay taxes twice on the same money.

SUPPLIES/INSTRUMENTS—Supplies and instruments sold to the buyer have already been written off, or expensed, by the seller. Therefore, they will be treated as ordinary income to the seller and can be written off or expensed by the buyer in the year of the sale.

EQUIPMENT—Allocating a portion of the purchase price to the equipment is the only area where buyer and seller have different objectives, taxwise. Because the seller has already, most likely, depreciated the equipment (written it off over a period of time) and had the tax deductions for so doing, now if the equipment is sold, the amount received for that equipment depreciation has to be recaptured, which means that the amount deducted has to be paid back, which results in the amount allocated being treated as ordinary income. However, if the amount allocated exceeds the amount depreciated (written off), the excess over and above the depreciated value will be treated as a capital gain.

The reason this becomes somewhat of a conflict is that the buyer wants as much allocated to the equipment as possible because he or she can depreciate it over a very short period of time, usually five to seven years or can take advantage of the Section 179, an accelerated tax deduction, and a large amount of the equipment allocation can be written off in the first year of the purchase.

Again, because everyone has different tax situations, it is critical that your tax advisor is informed and aware of how the allocations are being made in order to optimize your individual tax treatment come tax time. A mistake in this area *cannot* be corrected after the fact, because, as mentioned before, the IRS requires that a Form 8594 be completed by both buyer and seller and submitted with their regular taxes, and both of these forms have got to have the identical allocations. It is very easy for a computer to pick up discrepancies in the numbers, and it will automatically raise the red audit flag.

PATIENT RECORDS—Patient records are usually not allocated separately because they are, in fact, the goodwill. The seller receives capital gain treatment, and the buyer can amortize or write the allocated value off over a fifteen-year period.

GOODWILL—Goodwill is treated as a capital gain for the seller and is amortized over fifteen years for the buyer. It is important to make the distinction between corporate and personal goodwill at this time. When selling a practice that is incorporated or an LLC/LLP, it is important that the goodwill be identified as the dentist's personal goodwill and not that of the practice. This is especially important in the sale of a C corporation, in that the assets of the corporation are taxed twice, once at the corporate level and a second time when the income is received by the dentist from the corporation. Since the goodwill is usually the largest allocation in the sale, this can become a very expensive mistake if not properly allocated.

CONSULTING AGREEMENT—Consulting agreements are treated as ordinary income for the seller and are deductible as paid by the buyer. A consulting agreement is just another type of employment agreement and is therefore treated the same. In some cases where the seller is staying as an associate after the sale and is continuing to fund a defined benefit retirement plan (which requires the participant to be employed), a consulting agreement may be requested by the seller's financial advisor. It should be cautioned, however, that as long as capital gains taxes are at 15%, it is questionable to put money into a defined benefit plan in an effort to defer taxes because when the money is taken out of the plan, it will be taxed at the 35% or ordinary income tax rate. It seems wiser to take the money, pay the 15% capital gains tax, and then invest it in some form of tax-free instruments such as municipal bonds.

It is also not a bad idea, if the seller is incorporated, to have the corporation as an independent contractor of the seller, thus avoiding some of the payroll taxes for the buyer, and the seller can use the corporation to shelter certain expenses for tax purposes.

DEFERRED COMPENSATION—Deferred compensation, or an income shift, is treated as ordinary income to the seller and as pre-tax or tax-free dollars to the buyer. Deferred compensation is usually used for buy-ins to a corporation or LLC/LLP in order for the buyer to be able to get favorable tax treatment.

There are two reasons for using deferred compensation in a transition. First, lenders will not loan money for a buy-in, or partial sale of a practice without the entire practice being put up as collateral for the loan. Most sellers are unwilling to expose the entire value of the practice as collateral, so the buyer can borrow the buy-in money. Therefore, buy-ins are, almost always, financed by the seller. And second, if the seller practice is a corporation, the buyer has to purchase stock to buy into the practice, and he or she is not able to write the stock off.

Therefore, to get to a win-win situation for the buyer and the seller, the buyer will purchase the stock in the corporation for a nominal amount of money and then take a reduced income from the corporation for a determined period of time, leaving that money in the corporation, money which is then paid to the seller as a management or consulting fee. However, the income received by the seller from the corporation as a management fee is now treated as ordinary income instead of capital gains, and therefore, the amount received by the seller has to be grossed up or increased to offset the difference between capital gains and ordinary income.

This may appear, at first blush, to be disadvantageous to the buyer because the purchase price has increased; however, it must be remembered that the buyer is not receiving the money left in the corporation and is therefore not paying taxes on it. So, in effect, the largest portion of the goodwill purchase will be with pre-tax dollars. In other words, if the buyer was paying for the buy-in with a note, he or she would receive his or her pay, pay the taxes on the amount received, and then write a check to the seller, thus paying the ordinary income tax rate on the money *be-*

fore paying the seller. With the deferred compensation, the buyer never sees that money and therefore pays no taxes on it, which effectively lowers the purchase price.

Obviously, this type of transaction is very complicated and requires someone with the knowledge and experience in structuring the deferred compensation buy-in. The calculations are significantly complicated so that, very often, even accountants and attorneys who perform transition work do not engage in these types of transactions. It is critical that you use the right experts to assist in this process.

RESTRICTIVE COVENANT—Often referred to as a covenant not to compete, a restrictive covenant is usually required by the buyer in the sale of a dental practice. Alabama is the only state that does not allow restrictive covenants in the sale of a business. The amount of money allocated to the restrictive covenant is treated as ordinary income to the seller and can be written off over a fifteen-year period by the buyer. Because a restrictive covenant is ordinary income to the seller, most sellers and their advisors want to reduce this allocated amount. However, the buyer and his or her advisors may want a substantial amount allocated to discourage the seller from violating the covenant.

The win-win solution to this conflict is to not allocate a specific amount to the restrictive covenant but to include the restrictive covenant agreement as an addendum to the purchase and sale agreement, which makes it part of the agreement. From there, include language that indicates that the transaction would not have been entered into without the restrictive covenant, and therefore the entire purchase price of the practice would be considered as damages in the event of a breach of the restrictive covenant. This certainly would discourage a breach by the seller and eliminates the ordinary income treatment of the restrictive covenant, allowing a greater amount to be allocated to goodwill which, again, is treated as a capital gain.

Should, however, a buyer demand a certain amount be allocated to the restrictive covenant, and that amount is a nominal amount, it could be ruled by the court that the damages to be paid for the breach of that covenant would be the amount paid for it. In other words, if someone pays $800,000 for a practice and the buyer's attorney demands that at least $10,000 be allocated to the restrictive covenant to "avoid scrutiny by the IRS" (which is the common fear, however, with no basis in fact), and the seller sets up across the street in violation of the restrictive covenant, a valid argument would be that the buyer paid $10,000 for the restrictive covenant and, as the seller, he will pay the $10,000 back and continue practicing. Not an enviable position for the new buyer of a practice to be in!

STOCK—As earlier stated, stock receives capital gains treatment to the seller (it must be held at least one year for long-term capital gains treatment) but is not deductible to the buyer, nor is the interest paid (if the money to buy the stock was borrowed) allowed to be written off, because you cannot write off interest for money borrowed to buy securities.

Therefore, buying stock is not a desirable option for the buyer. However, in a buy-in situation, into a corporation or an LLC/LLP, the only way to buy in is to buy stock.

It is in this circumstance where we use deferred compensation to accomplish a favorable tax result for both the buyer and the seller.

In a straight sale of a practice, the corporation is never purchased, and therefore the stock is not sold. In the total sale of a practice that is incorporated, the assets of the corporation (equipment, supplies, furnishings, etc.) and the personal goodwill of the dentist seller are sold independently as separate allocations. The corporation can continue to exist if the seller so chooses, or it can be dissolved, but the buyer, if he or she wants to be incorporated, will set up a new corporation.

Solo Group

The solo group concept is a particularly attractive model for the multi-dentist practice. It provides all of the advantages of working in a group setting without the disadvantages that contribute to so many partnership dissolution problems.

The solo group allows for a dentist to sell a portion (any portion from 5% to 95%) of his practice to another dentist, retain the remaining portion, then share space, equipment, some staff, and utilities. It also provides the mentoring/consulting opportunity and the time-off coverage that so many solo practitioners do not have. This model of sharing reduces overhead but still allows for complete autonomy and independence for each dentist.

The ideal development of a solo group starts at the beginning of a relationship, creating separate patient bases for each dentist, establishing separate phone numbers and keeping individual financial statements and bank accounts. However, the solo group usually evolves out of an existing practice and therefore is "carved out," which requires more effort in the separation of patients and staff.

The basic concept requires that each dentist have a

separate patient base (no commingling or cross-treating of patients), a separate telephone number, separate income and expense statements, and separate staff members. In most cases, some staff can be shared, such as front desk and hygiene, but the true solo group has completely separate and independent practices that function under one roof.

The development process is specifically defined and usually takes from two to three years to achieve. Because each practice is different, it requires careful analysis of the practice, clear understanding of the goals and objectives of each of the dentists, and realistic projections that are generated from existing practice data. Once this information has been gathered and analyzed, a plan can be prepared and agreements entered into that will ultimately culminate in two separate practices operating side by side, with coverage, mentoring/consulting availability, and reduced overhead.

Once again, because creating the solo group is not a cookie-cutter process, it requires someone with the skill, experience, and expertise to provide the guidance to plan, develop the solo group concept, and bring it to successful fruition.

The beauty of the solo group is that in the event of partnership incompatibility (clinical, personal, professional, or social), either dentist can pick up and take his or her practice next door or across the street with no damage to either practice.

Because of the time required to establish a solo group, this model is not usually a practical model for a dentist with a five-year or less exit strategy. However, if the exit strategy is eight to fifteen years or more, the practice is growing to the point that additional dentists are needed or desired, and the facility is of adequate size to accommodate another practice, the solo group is an ideal transition mechanism.

As an added advantage, the solo group can also be structured to provide for the buyout by the other practice in the event of death or disability.

Transition Planning and Requirements

In this chapter, we will summarize and outline what is needed and what to expect when buying or selling a dental practice.

TIME—The time it takes to sell a dental practice can be from three months to three years. A lot of the timing issues depend on the market demand in a particular area. It is interesting that those states that have opened up their borders to reciprocity generally have a much shorter turnaround time for those sellers than those that are restricted to state licensure issues. Most of the closed states try to restrict the number of dentists practicing in the state, and therefore often have politically motivated dental boards that can seem discriminatory to dentists who want to practice in that state, often restricting very qualified dentists from becoming potential buyers of practices for sale.

VALUE—The first step in any transition is determining the value of the practice. This will require some kind of valuation or appraisal. As stated in the beginning of this book, there are different approaches to value and different levels of appraisals, from the verbal opinion of value to the full appraisal with a comprehensive report. Though an inexpensive or free verbal opinion of value may satisfy your curiosity, it may not meet the requirements of a potential buyer or a buyer's lender. Therefore, the first step to take is to get an official appraisal with a comprehensive written report that supports and justifies the value conclusions reached. A letter appraisal, though written, does not support, with data, the value arrived at and is really not any more valuable than a verbal opinion, regardless of who provides the opinion. You can't take it to the bank!

Once you have the appraisal in hand, it is important to realize and accept that the value stated is probably the *most* that you will receive for your practice, and with this information, you can evaluate the economics of selling for that price. If you had anticipated and needed more than the appraised value, you may be better off staying a little longer, working to increase the value, and making more contributions to your retirement, until you reach that financial freedom point that allows you to retire.

Most appraisals, in addition to a numerical value, will give you information that will help you see the weaknesses in your practice. This information gives you the opportunity to improve the value of the practice by making the necessary adjustments.

FINDING A BUYER—Assuming the value of the practice is acceptable, now you need to find a buyer. Very often, this step happens unexpectedly, and you need to backtrack to get the appraisal done. In any case, once a buyer has been identified, the negotiation process begins. This process can be simple or complex, friendly or hostile; but at some point, you will either agree on the basic terms and conditions, or you will not. Because of the dynamics of a practice sale, all of the terms and conditions will not be agreed to in the beginning because there are too many issues to resolve. Therefore, the basic terms and conditions of the transition should be agreed to, and the rest of the items will be settled one at a time as the process continues.

INITIAL AGREEMENT—The four issues that should be agreed to in the beginning are purchase price, method of payment (cash at closing or seller financing or a combination thereof), closing date, and terms of the restrictive covenant. Once these terms and conditions have been agreed to, we have a meeting of the minds on these issues. This does not mean that we have a deal; it just means that we have a solid foundation for a deal to work from.

At this point, the seller and buyer should execute a letter of intent that outlines the agreed-upon terms and conditions, and the buyer should make an earnest money deposit. It does not have to be a large sum, and it will be refundable in the event the transaction does not close.

From the time of signing a letter of intent to closing usually takes from forty-five to ninety days, although the timeline can be stretched, if necessary. During this time, all of the other terms and conditions of the transaction will be worked out and the financing commitment procured.

The buy-in, partnership, or solo group structure will take significantly longer because the buyer has got to be established and generating significant production before he or she can afford the buy-in. The documentation required is also totally different and more complicated than for the straight sale. However, the same initial process should be followed. An appraisal and projected buy-in price should be agreed upon, whether it is an actual dollar amount or some formula, such as percentage of gross or net. There should also be some form of projecting at what point, productionwise, the buyer can afford to buy into the practice, and with this projection, a general time frame during which it seems practical that the buyer can achieve this goal.

DOCUMENTS—The documents required for a transition depend on the type of transaction.

- An outright sale will require a purchase and sale agreement, restrictive covenant and/or non-solicitation agreement, lease, bill of sale, and closing statements.

- A buy-in to a corporation will require a stock purchase agreement, revision of the corporation shareholder agreement, minutes reflecting the action of the board of directors, and employment agreements with each of the dentists of the corporation.

- A buy-in with a defined buyout would require the same documents as the buy-in, but would also provide for the obligation, options, or rights of first refusal for the buyout. These provisions may include formulas or actual numbers for the purchase price, time frames, payment terms, and so on. Usually at the buyout, the buyer will again pay a nominal fee for the stock (for tax purposes), which will include the tangible assets (they will most likely be owned by the corporation) and the balance of the purchase price allocated to the personal goodwill of the selling dentist. The buyout will be a cash transaction because the buyer will be able to get financing by collateralizing the entire practice. The buyout will still be a win-win transaction because the seller will receive capital gains treatment for the entire sale price, and the buyer will be able to amortize the value of the goodwill over a fifteen-year period.

- The solo group requires an initial agreement with the entire process defined, including the way each dentist's patients will be transferred and identified, protection of each dentist's individual goodwill, the purchase price (dollars or formulas), and approximate time frame for the buyout point. The buyout point is established in the beginning of the relationship and is projected as a function of the income and expenses of the practice as well as the number of active patients, the number of new patients, staffing requirements, and the facility. At the buyout, the same documents as for an outright sale are required since, in fact, there is an outright sale of goodwill and a fifty percent undivided interest in the tangible assets (equipment and supplies).

Definition and Function of the Documents:

Confidentiality Agreement

A confidentiality agreement is often required by the seller or the seller's advisor or broker before identifying a practice and providing the proprietary information about the practice. This agreement is a legal and enforceable agreement that can have serious financial implications if damage occurs to the practice because information is distributed that should not be made available to the public at large.

Letter of Intent

A letter of intent is usually a nonbinding agreement that describes the basic terms and conditions of the transaction. As mentioned above, it should include the agreed-upon purchase price, method of payment, restrictive covenant parameters, and closing date, and it should be accompanied by a refundable earnest money deposit by the buyer.

Purchase and Sale Agreement

The purchase and sale agreement will identify all of the terms and conditions of the sale, including the allocations of the various assets, the payment terms, restrictive covenant parameters, closing date, and indemnification language. It will be a very comprehensive document and should be drafted specifically for the sale of a dental practice, not a generic agreement used for any business transaction. There are issues that are very dental-specific that should be included in this document, therefore requiring someone with knowledge of your state dental act to make sure that the required issues are addressed.

Restrictive Covenant

The restrictive covenant will restrict a party to the transaction, usually the seller, from practicing dentistry or associating with a dental practice in any capacity within a certain area and for a certain period of time after leaving the practice. The time and distance criteria are jurisdictional, meaning that every court jurisdiction will have set acceptable standards of time and distance that they deem reasonable. In the event the restrictions are challenged or breached and the issue ends up in litigation, the court may determine whether the restrictions are too severe. They may also disallow the covenant altogether or revise it to meet the acceptable reasonable standard set by the jurisdiction. Though the restrictive covenant time and distance is usually defined in the purchase and sale agreement, a separate restrictive covenant agreement should be attached to the purchase and sale agreement as an addendum, which makes it part of the purchase and sale agreement. The restrictive covenant agreement should be a complete, stand-alone agreement that is comprehensive in nature and defines all of the terms and conditions of the restrictions agreed to, including the penalties and remedies for breach of the agreement.

Reverse Restrictive Covenant

A reverse restrictive covenant is appropriate in the event the seller is financing all or part of the transaction. The reverse restrictive covenant protects the seller in the event the buyer defaults on his or her payment obligations and restricts him or her from practicing in a competitive area in order to protect the seller's practice.

Promissory Note

A promissory note is the legal document that obligates the executer of the note to pay the holder of the note the money owed. Usually the only time a promissory note is involved between a buyer and seller is if the seller is financing the transaction. A buyer will be executing a promissory note with whomever he or she has borrowed the money, whether the seller or a commercial lender. There should only be *one* copy of the promissory note actually executed. With the other legal documents, multiple copies can be signed with original signatures, and in fact, should be. But there should be only one original signed copy of the promissory note with copies made of the original that are clearly marked as copies.

Security Agreement

The security agreement is the document that secures the promissory note. It reiterates the terms and conditions of the financial obligation, the terms of payment, the collateral supporting the value of the note, and the penalties in the event of default on the note. A security agreement should always accompany a promissory note so that the holder of the note will have adequate recourse in the event of a default.

Closing Statements

The closing statements, usually one for the seller and one for the buyer, identify the way the money in the transaction was disbursed. Closing statements are necessary for determining tax issues when the tax returns are filed and should be signed by all parties to the transaction, verifying that the money that was disbursed to the buyer, seller, and third parties, was, in fact, agreed to by all the parties to the transaction.

Employment Agreement

Any time there is an entity, such as a corporation, LLC/LLP, or partnership, there should be employment agreements with each of the principals in the entity. This includes the solo dentist that is incorporated. The employment agreement should, at minimum, include a job description and compensation provisions. When there is more than one dentist in an entity, it is imperative to have employment agreements that define the obligations of each dentist to the corporation and the corporation's responsibilities to the dentist, including compensation and benefits. There should also be provisions for termination in the event of violations of "moral turpitude" (dishonesty, illegal activity, immoral behavior, etc.), the loss of license, or disability to the extent they cannot practice.

Independent Contractor Agreement

In some cases, an independent contractor relationship is engaged; however, the definitions for a true independent contractor relationship are very specific and clearly defined by the IRS. The reason the IRS is involved in defining a true independent contractor is because the independent contractor relationship is too often established to avoid paying payroll taxes. Some of the requirements that identify a true independent contractor are; the contractor sets his or her own schedule, has his or her own patients, sets charges and collects fees independently, uses his or her own tools, and keeps separate financial statements. There are other criteria that also must be met, but if the practice is setting the dentist's schedule and setting and collecting fees for the services rendered by the associate dentist, the relationship is automatically *not* an independent contractor relationship and if audited, will be disallowed, which will most likely result in penalties and interest for delinquent payroll taxes. An example of a true independent contractor would be a general dentist who leases space to an endodontist where the endodontist sets the fees and the schedule and brings his own equipment to the practice. The penalties, if caught, are not worth the risk.

Shareholder Agreement

The shareholder agreement is, or should be, a part of the corporate documents in a C or Subchapter S corporation. The shareholder agreement defines the ownership in the corporation, the operating conditions in the corporation, and the dissolution provisions, including insurance requirements and buyout agreements between the parties. It is not infrequent that the shareholder agreement is either found to be incomplete with respect to all of the necessary terms and conditions of the parties' agreements, or is woefully neglected and never updated. Along with the corporate minutes, which should be, by law, updated every year at the annual shareholder meeting (which is also often disregarded), the shareholder agreement should be updated and revised to meet the expectations of the shareholders. In some cases, the agreements are not even signed, which renders them invalid in the event of a litigious dissolution.

Operating Agreement

The operating agreement plays the same function in the LLC/LLP as the shareholder agreement in the corporation. Once again, it should be updated regularly and contain the provisions that the members of the LLC/LLP desire as far as ownership, operating relationship, and dissolution provisions.

ADVISORS—The advisors that are a *must* in any of these transactions are:

Attorney

The attorney chosen to represent you in these transactions should be a deal maker and have experience in dental practice transitions, including the state dental act requirements and the tax laws. It is unfortunate, but many lawyers are resentful of consultants and/or brokers who provide boiler plate legal documents to their clients. Because the brokers are on the front lines daily, they are up to date on the tax issues, the market issues, and the legal issues that relate to their brokerage or consulting practice. Most attorneys may only provide these services once or twice in their career unless they specialize in dental practice law. There are several attorneys in the country who specialize in dental legal services and do an excellent job for their clients. Beware, however, of those attorneys who do not specialize in dental practice law who want to totally rewrite the agreements or renegotiate the deal. This will kill a transaction faster than anything else.

Accountant

Usually the seller has an established relationship with an accountant or CPA. Often, the buyer does not. Accountants are usually engaged to prepare financial statements and do taxes. The sale of a dental practice is totally different and requires a different approach and often, different tax knowledge. Like attorneys, accountants rarely get involved in the sale of a dental practice and therefore know little about market forces or transactional data. A good accountant is also being as creative as is legal to *reduce* your net income for tax purposes, therefore potentially impacting the value of the practice. Most accountants are very easy to work with, but again, once in a while, there will be one who defies all the experts and demands certain structures that may severely impact the transaction or the tax consequences of the transaction. Remember, *you* are employing your attorney and accountant. They are not employing you! You should be able to tell them that this is the deal that you want to do and ask them to point out to you any issues that they might be concerned about. But you, ultimately, should make the decision, not the attorney or the accountant.

Brokers and Consultants

Like any professionals, there are very good and very bad brokers and consultants with a lot of mediocre ones in between. There are very honest and ethical brokers and consultants who can be of incredible value to you in your transition, but you should spend the time to seek them out. As is often said about lawyers, "The most expensive lawyer is a cheap lawyer." The same goes for brokers and consultants. You will get what you pay, for and the industry is small enough that it does not take much investigation and inquiry to find out who does a good job and knows their business and those who do not. Dentists do not like paying a commission to a broker or consultant, but choosing the right broker will more than pay for itself, not only in the quality of the service that you receive, but also in actual dollars you save and/or receive for the services rendered. One of the most accurate ways to identify a good broker or consultant is to talk to the commercial lenders who provide loans for dental practice sales. They do business with most of the brokers and will provide you with references they do business with. Remember, they are lending a lot of money in these transactions and need to do good deals that are successful. They know who they can trust when it comes to quality and integrity.

Lenders

As a buyer, at some point in the process, you will most likely need to borrow money, and as a business person, establishing a relationship with a reputable third-party financial institution will be essential. The initial relationship when purchasing a practice is important because it will determine the terms and conditions of the loan, which include the interest rate, the time over which the loan will be paid back, the amount of money that can be borrowed, and the availability of working capital and the future availability of money for growth and/or expansion and new equipment. To establish this partnership with the right lender is important. Lenders are not all the same, and some seem very willing to make the loan as easy as possible for you by extending the term out or even deferring payments. It is not prudent to borrow more money than is needed nor to extend the loan period longer than is required. It will only cost you more than necessary in the long run. Remember, lenders make their money by lending it to you. The higher the interest rate and/or the longer the loan, the more money they make. Because you can save total interest charges by paying the loan off quicker than scheduled, the lender may impose penalties for early payment to assure that they make the amount of money they want to make.

One of the biggest mistakes made by borrowers is

overreacting to the interest rates. Remember that a practice acquisition loan is not collateralized like a home loan. In other words, if you default on your house payment, the bank can sell your house to recover their money. With a dental practice, however, the majority of the value is in the goodwill, and therefore, the only thing the bank can really sell is the equipment, which is usually valued at a fraction of the whole practice value. The good news is that very few—less than 0.05%—of dental practices fail, and therefore, the lenders are on pretty solid ground when they lend for the purchase of a practice. The other thing to remember is that this is a business loan and not a home mortgage, so interest rates are going to be higher. Often, the first-time buyer of a practice is surprised by the interest rate because they are familiar with the home mortgage rates and assume them to be the same. We talked about cash flow earlier, and you will remember that debt service (the loan to purchase the practice) was one of the components. When cash flowing a practice (overhead, officers' compensation, and debt service), it is standard to amortize the loan (the period of the loan) over a seven-year period. If it can be paid off earlier, that is even better, but for cash flow purposes, seven years should be used. If it has to be stretched out for a longer period of time, either the price is too high or the interest rates are too high. Some lenders want to provide you with a period of six to twelve months on the front end of the loan with no payments due. This will create negative amortization, which is nothing more than interest being charged on interest, which in the long run can significantly increase the total amount of interest you pay for the money you borrow. Remember, any practice will cash flow if the loan is extended out long enough!

But, like credit cards, if the minimum due is all that is paid it might take forty years to pay off the present existing balance. The following chart will show the total amount paid in interest using the same interest rate but with different payment periods.

Principal Amount	$500,000	$500,000	$500,000	$500,000
Interest Rate	8.5%	8.5%	8.5%	8.5%
Term	7 Yrs (84 Mos.)	10 Yrs (120 Mos.)	15 Yrs (180 Mos.)	18 Yrs (216 Mos.)
Monthly Payment	$7,918	$6,199	$4,924	$4,527
Total Interest Paid	$165,132	$243,914	$386,266	$477,895
Total Cost of Loan	$665,132	$743,914	$886,266	$977,895
Cost Difference		$(78,781)	$(221,134)	$(312,763)

When carefully thought through, you can see the difference in payments between a seven-year loan and an eighteen-year loan is $3,391 per month. That means that if you do one extra crown per week, you will pay for the difference and save $312,763 in interest payments. And just to make you think about that one year with no payments, the additional amount of interest that you will pay will be $36,000.

DISSOLUTION PROVISIONS—Just a comment about dissolution provisions: regardless of the model that you choose for a multi-doctor relationship, the "stepchild" of provisions in the documents, whether it is a partnership, a corporation or an LLC/LLP are the dissolution provisions that kick in when the relationship dissolves. All relationships ultimately dissolve! Whether because of retirement, disability, death, or personal conflicts, all relationships ultimately end. It is therefore critical that the dissolution provisions covering any and all contingencies be defined in depth before the fact and not at the point of dissolution. Most dissolutions are not amicable dissolutions, regardless of reason. Therefore, these provisions must be incorporated when the parties are in a compatible stage of their relationship, and the best time is at the beginning, when the initial documents are drafted. As mentioned before, these provisions should be re-evaluated and assessed every year so that the necessary changes can be made and incorporated into the documents.

For sellers, it is very probable that if you think through your goals and objectives, understand your retirement requirements, evaluate honestly your practice and your exit strategy, and—most of all—use advisors who understand dentistry and the transition process, you will experience a successful and profitable transition.

For buyers, find the best and most experienced consultants and brokers and trust their knowledge and expertise. Consult with bankers who work with brokers every day to find those you can trust to keep your interests and concerns in mind. By surrounding yourself with the best advisors and listening to their advice and counsel, you will not make a mistake. Remember, this is a *life decision*, and it should be taken very seriously.

Appendices

Several additional documents are enclosed in the appendixes of this book. One is a codicil. A codicil is an attachment to a last will and testament that provides legal instructions that sidestep probate in the event of an unexpected death of a dentist. The codicil identifies a person or entity that is instructed to manage, operate, and dispose of the practice. In times of bereavement, all of the family members are under extreme stress and pressure, including family attorneys and practice staff members. Trying to run the practice and make decisions about its operation and/ or disposal is, initially, relatively low on the priority list, but if not handled properly, can create serious problems for the practice and preserving its value for the estate.

Also included is a checklist that assists in the gathering of information that should be available in the event of an unexpected death or catastrophic disability. This gift to those left in charge of putting all of the pieces together will simplify that onerous responsibility. This expanded checklist was originally provided by John Cahill of Western Practice Sales, an ADS affiliate in Northern California. There are several consultants, including my firm and John

Cahill's, that provide death and disability preparation programs that are very useful.

A buyer's checklist is also included, which will assist the buyer in making sure all of the many considerations in buying a practice are evaluated and considered.

A seller's checklist is also included, which provides information that needs to be gathered for the marketing and financing of the sale of the practice.

Finally, a glossary of terms is included to help both buyer and seller with some terms that are used by attorneys, accountants, brokers, and lenders. This glossary is provided by Ted Schumann, CPA, CFA, of DBS Companies, an ADS affiliate in Michigan.

Codicil

State of _____ County of _____

I, _____, order my Executor(s)
to appoint ADS FLORIDA, LLC, located at 999 Vanderbilt
Road, Suite 200, Naples, Florida 34108, to sell or otherwise
dispose of my dental practice located at _____
_____
or other subsequent address I may practice at, for the best
interests of my estate.

ADS FLORIDA, LLC, shall, without order of any court,
have the power to do all acts customary and necessary to
effectuate the sale or liquidation of my dental practice including continuing the operation of said practice so it may
be sold as a going concern.

If my dental practice is sold as a going concern, it is ex-
pressly agreed that, without detracting from the generality
of the foregoing, the following specific powers and exemp-
tions are included in this appointment:

1. ADS Florida, LLC, may contract with licensed dentists
    for continued practice operation.

2. ADS Florida, LLC, may continue employment of pres-

ent staff and employ replacements if resignations occur.

3. ADS Florida, LLC, may purchase dental supplies on open account or otherwise.

4. ADS Florida, LLC, may continue payment of office and equipment leases and notes.

Income from the continuing operation of my practice, after expenses, shall go to my estate in monthly installments.

ADS FLORIDA, LLC, shall be without liability for employees' actions or for any other losses of the practice provided it exercises reasonable care. ADS FLORIDA, LLC, shall be held harmless and defended or indemnified by my estate against all claims asserted against it by third parties.

Said sale or liquidation shall be completed within twelve (12) months of probate. Compensation for ADS FLORIDA, LLC, shall be ten percent (10%) of the selling price or Seven Thousand Five Hundred and No/100 Dollars ($7,500.00), whichever is greater.

So far as this Codicil creates inconsistent provisions in my will, this latter expression of my intent shall prevail.

IN WITNESS WHEREOF
I have hereunto set my hand and affixed my seal to this, my Codicil to my Will this the _____ day of _____, 201__.

Signed, sealed, published and declared by _____

while of sound mind, as and for a Codicil to his Last Will and Testament in our presence; and we, at his request and in his presence, and in the presence of each other have hereunto subscribed our names as Witnesses the day and year set out above.

WITNESSES: ADDRESS:

_____   _____

_____   _____

_____   _____

_____   _____

Instruction in the Event of Death

LETTER OF INSTRUCTION TO SPOUSE AND STAFF

<u>What to Include</u>

1. Label on outside—"Open Upon Death or Major Disability"

2. Copy to: Spouse/Attorney/Staff

3. Have Receptionist/Office Manager notify all other staff members

4. Office Manager/Receptionist should make contact with Spouse and/or surviving children for handling office.

5. Review Death/Disability Manual, if one exists

6. Contact Death/Disability Group, if in one

7. Contact Practice Broker, e.g., Hy Smith, MBA; Paul Rang, DMD, JD; Stuart M. Auerbach, DDS; Gregory Auerbach, MBA, at Professional Transitions, Inc.

8. Cancel patients for one (1) week, telling them of the death or disability

9. Arrange for emergencies to be seen by Death/Disability Group or another Dentist.

10. Complete and/or update Professional Transitions, Inc. Seller's Practice Profile and gather the attached list of documents to be forwarded to your local representative.

11. Notify the following people:
    a. Attorney
    b. Accountant
    c. Letters to patients
    i. When should they be sent?
    ii. What should patients be told?
    d. Letters to referring doctor, if applicable
    e. Malpractice carrier
    f. Closest professional colleague(s)
    g. Others: _____

12. What to do with practice income — checking/savings/money to spouse

13. Need for supplies to continue operations

14. Bills to be paid (will depend on office)

15. Arrange for delivery of lab cases

16. What work is to be started?

17. What should be done about new patients?

18. Complete exiting treatment plans

19. Complete an inventory of equipment

20. Complete an inventory of supplies

21. Where to locate assets, etc.

INFORMATION REQUIRED FOR MARKETING AND EVALUATING A PRACTICE

1. PTI Practice Profile (filled out completely)

2. Pension and retirement fund accounting records, as related to employees

3. Year-End Financial Statements for the past three (3) years including practice production/collections (by month) and expenses

4. Current Year-to-Date Profit and Loss Statements and Balance Sheet

5. Schedule C's from Personal Tax Returns for last three (3) years and any related or appropriate statements or Corporate Income Tax Returns for last three (3) years and any related or appropriate statements

6. Depreciation Schedule from the last Tax Return

7. Aging of accounts receivable (30/60/90/over)

8. Average daily hygiene production for the last three (3) years

9. Current list of major equipment; instruments and office furniture

10. Fee Schedule (most current)

11. If computerized, include a list of reports received each month or annually

12. Copy of Office Lease and Floor Plan (if available)

13. Any Lease Agreements on equipment, furniture and fixtures

14. List of any existing liens secured by the practice (e.g., bank loan)

15. List of Insurance, Union, or PPO contracts

16. Copy of any Office Policies (personnel policies)

17. Copy of cover page of your malpractice insurance policy

18. Current resume or Curriculum Vitae

19. Pictures of the practice

Seller's Checklist

_____ Complete Seller Profile
_____ 3 Yrs of Personal Tax Returns
_____ 3 Yrs of Financial Statements
_____ Provide Fee Schedule
_____ Provide Inventory

UPON LETTER OF INTENT EXECUTION
_____ Attorney
_____ Accountant
_____ Contracts preparation:
    _____ Purchase & Sale
    _____ Allocations
    _____ Inventory
    _____ Pre-paid Expenses & Deposits
    _____ Staff Benefits due
    _____ Liabilities (Yellow Pages, Computer Contracts, etc.)
    _____ Define Patient Re-treatment and Refund Policy
    _____ Restrictive Covenant
    _____ Time and Distance
    _____ Seller Note
    _____ Interest Rate and Period
    _____ Seller Security Agreement
_____ Seller Employment Agreement
    _____ Term and Compensation

_____ Contract for Real Estate
_____ Provide Lease
_____ Landlord Subordination Agreement
_____ Set Closing Date

DUE DILIGENCE
_____ Provide Tax Returns and Financial Statements
_____ Provide Fee Schedule
_____ Provide Employee Wages and Benefits
_____ Provide Employee Contracts
_____ Count Active Patient Records & Provide Charts
_____ Provide Appointment Book and Recall System
_____ Verify Monthly Collections with Bank Statements and Deposits
_____ Tangible Tax Bill

PRE-CLOSING
_____ Introduce New Dr. to Staff
_____ Approve Patient Announcement Letter
_____ Arrange payment or Credit of Employee Benefits
_____ Change Telephone Number
_____ Finish Cases in Progress
_____ Provide Payoff Letters from Creditors

POST-CLOSING
_____ Terminate Professional Liability Insurance
_____ Terminate Office Insurance
_____ Notify Dental Authorities of New Status
_____ Change Merchant Credit Card Account

Buyer's Checklist

I. UPON SIGNING LETTER OF INTENT

____ Complete Purchaser Profile, Credit Authorization, Personal Financial Statement

____ Submit Loan Application and Financing Requests

____ Provide 3 years of personal tax returns

____ Current income documentation (Paystub)

____ Copy of malpractice insurance

____ Copy of driver's license

____ Copy of Green Card (if applicable)

____ Copy of Florida dental license

____ Copy of DEA license

____ Copy of life and disability policies

____ Articles of Incorporation (if incorporated)

____ Retain Attorney

____ Retain Accountant

____ Contracts Preparation:

____ Purchase & Sale Agreement

____ Allocation of Purchase Price

____ Inventory

____ Pre-paid Expenses & Deposits

____ Liabilities (Yellow Pages, computer, maintenance contracts, etc.)

____ Restrictive Covenant

____ Seller Note and Security Agreement (if applicable)

____ Seller Employment Agreement (if applicable)

____ Term and Compensation (if applicable)

____ Contract for Real Estate (if applicable)
____ Office Lease (assignment or new lease)
____ Landlord Subordination Agreement
____ Insurance
____ Professional Liability (malpractice)
____ Life
____ Disability &/or Office Overhead
____ Casualty, Fire, Flood & Windstorm
____ Office Premises Liability
____ Unemployment
____ Workers Compensation

2. DUE DILIGENCE
____ Review Tax Returns and Financial Statements
____ Review Fee Schedule
____ Review Employee Contracts, Wages and Benefits
____ Count Active Patient Records and Review Charts
____ Review Appointment Book and Recall System
____ Verify Monthly Collections with Bank Statements and Deposits
____ Review Tangible Tax Bill
____ Review Insurance Programs (PPO, HMO, Medicaid)

3. PRE-CLOSING
____ Return Signed Financing Documents to Lender
____ Meet with Staff
____ Prepare Patient Announcement Letter
____ Assignment of life insurance
____ Assignment of disability and/or office overhead insurance
____ Loss payable on fire and casualty insurance
____ Obtain Federal Tax ID #

____ Open Bank Checking Account
____ Open Merchant Credit Card Account
____ Order:
____ Supplies Business Cards Prescription Pads Station-
ary
____ Newspaper Announcement
____ Yellow Pages Ad
____ Set Closing Date
____ Apply for Insurance Programs (PPO, HMO, Medic-
aid)

4. POST-CLOSING
____ Licenses and Permits
____ Dental Societies (State & Local)
____ X-Ray notification
____ DEA License
____ Local and County Business/Occupational Licenses
____ Change Responsible Party for Telephone Number
and Utilities
____ Send Patient Announcement Letter

Glossary

A

Above-the-line Deduction

A term used to describe those deductions that the Internal Revenue Service allows a taxpayer to subtract from his or her gross income. A taxpayer's gross income minus his or her above-the-line deductions is equal to the adjusted gross income. Because these deductions are taken before adjusted gross income is calculated, they are termed "above the line."

Accounting

Recording and reporting of financial transactions, including the origination of the transaction, its recognition, processing, and summarization in the Financial Statements.

Accounts Receivable

Claim against a Debtor for an uncollected amount, generally from a completed transaction of sales or services rendered.

Accounts Receivable Aging

A method used by accountants and investors to evaluate and identify any irregularities within a company's account receivables. Aging is achieved by sorting and inspecting the accounts according to their length outstanding.

Accrued Interest

Interest that has been earned but not yet received or recorded.

Acid Test Ratio

The ratio of current assets less inventories to total current liabilities.

Active Patient

An active patient is one who has been in the practice for either re-care or operative treatment in a given time period. The professional standard for an active patient is eighteen to twenty-four months. However, a more conservative count will illustrate more clearly the core of the patient base, those who come in on a regular basis for their re-care appointments. ADS Florida uses an eighteen-month time period to define an active patient.

Advisors, Attorneys, Accountants

An expert who gives advice in their defined area of professional expertise.

Agency

The condition of being in action; operation. The means or mode of acting; instrumentality. A business or service authorized to act for others. In the sale or acquisition of a practice, agency is the relationship between a person (the **Principal**) and another person (the **Agent**) who was appointed, selected, empowered, given authority by the Principal to represent the interests of the Principal in dealings with third parties, and to bind the Principal to statements, warranties or contracts.

Agent

Amortization
Liquidation of debt through periodic payments over a specified period of time.

Amortization of Intangibles
A tax term relating to the practice of deducting the cost of an investment in a qualifying intangible asset over the projected life of the asset. The cost basis of the qualifying intangible asset is amortized over a fifteen-year period, irrespective of the actual useful life of the asset.

Amortization Schedule
A complete schedule of periodic blended loan payments, showing the amount of principal and the amount of interest that comprise each payment so that the loan will be paid off at the end of its term. Early in the schedule, the majority of each periodic payment is interest. Later in the schedule, the majority of each periodic payment is put toward the principal.

Annuity

An annuity is a contract between an insurance company and an individual in which the company agrees to provide an income, either fixed or variable, for a specified period of time.

Allocation of Price

To set apart for a special purpose; designate: to distribute according to a plan; allot. In a dental transition, this refers to the total sale/acquisition price of a practice and how the sale proceeds are defined within the given tax classes for beneficial tax treatment for both buyer and seller. This allocation must be mutually acceptable and reported to the Internal Revenue Service as part of the tax return filed by the buyer and seller respectively in the year of the sale.

Appraisal or Valuation of (Practice)

The formalized/written report of a given property, business, real estate, or equipment with respect to its worth. There is no one form of appraisal or valuation that is universally accepted. There are several appraisal and valuation methods in use and may be used in combination to ascertain a range of values and then the target value: Asset Method, Capitalization Of Excess Earnings, Market Comparables, Bank Proof, and Acid Test.

Appraisal—Building

The formalized/written report for given property with respect to its worth. In real estate, sales of property, and buildings, the market comparable sales approach is highly influential. Building appraisals should be done by a certified appraiser rather than a real estate agent.

Appraisal—Equipment

The formalized/written report of a given property, business, real estate, or equipment with respect to its worth. There are several types of value, and there must be clarity as to what value is used: book value, in-place value, depreciated value, new equipment, used equipment, and so forth.

Appreciation

An increase in value or price of an asset gained over term of ownership.

APR (Annual Percentage Rate)

The annual rate that is charged for borrowing (or made by investing), expressed as a single percentage number that represents the actual yearly cost of funds over the term of a loan. This includes any fees or additional costs associated with the transaction.

Asset

Anything an individual or business owns that has commercial or exchange value.

Asset-based Lender

A lender who bases loans by securing an asset. Therefore, if the loan is not repaid, the asset that is securing the loan is forfeited to the lender.

Asset Purchase Agreement

The detailed purchase agreement between the seller of a practice and the prospective buyer of the same practice. This contract will be specific to the two parties for the specific transaction and represents the wishes of the parties.

Asset Sale

A sale transaction that is based on the sale of individual specific assets, such as equipment, supplies, records, leasehold improvements, goodwill, and covenant versus the sale of stock in a corporation.

Asset Value

The net market value of a corporation's assets on a per share basis, not the market value of the shares. A company is undervalued in the market when asset value exceeds market value.

Associate

In dentistry, an associate is a doctor who is employed to perform dental treatment for a given practice under specific terms agreed to by the parties and defined in a contract. Generally, there will be a restrictive covenant and/or nonsolicitation clause as part of the agreement.

Associateship Agreement

A legal and binding contract between a host/ employing doctor and the doctor hired to work in the practice. In many states, the agreement must meet certain criteria to be enforceable.

Associate Buy-in

A sale transaction that involves the sale of a portion of the host/employing doctor's practice to the associate doctor, which, in turn, makes them partners.

Associate Buyout

A sale transaction that involves the sale of a portion of the host/employing doctor's practice to the associate doctor in which the host/employing doctor no longer has ownership in the practice.

B

Balance

The amount owed on a loan or credit card, or the amount of money in a savings or investment account.

Balance Sheet

A financial statement that provides an overview of the assets, liabilities, and net worth of a person or organization.

Below-the-line Deduction

Itemized deductions such as charitable donations and medical, tax, interest, and miscellaneous expenses.

Benchmark

A standard against which the performance of a security, mutual fund, or investment manager can be measured. Generally, broad market and market segment stock and bond indexes are used for this purpose.

DJIA

Dow Jones Industrial Average. The most widely used indicator of the overall condition of the stock market, a price-weighted average of thirty actively traded blue-chip stocks, primarily industrials. The thirty stocks are chosen by the editors of the *Wall Street Journal* (which is published by Dow Jones & Company). The Dow is computed using a price-weighted indexing system. Simply put, the editors at WSJ add up the prices of all the stocks and then divide by the number of stocks in the index. (In actuality, the divisor is much higher today in order to account for stock splits that have occurred in the past.)

S&P 500
Standard & Poor's 500. A basket of 500 stocks that are considered to be widely held. The S&P 500 index is weighted by market value, and its performance is thought to be representative of the stock market as a whole. This index provides a broad snapshot of the overall U.S. equity market; in fact, over 70% of all U.S. equity is tracked by the S&P 500. The index selects its companies based upon their market size, liquidity, and sector.

Russell 2000
The best-known of a series of market-value weighted indices published by the Frank Russell Company. The index measures the performance of the smallest 2,000 companies in the Russell 3000 Index of the 3,000 largest U.S. companies in terms of market capitalization.

EAFE
Europe, Australia, Far East. A regional area comprised of Europe, Australia, and the Far East. The Europe,

Australia, and Far East index is a way of investing in these regional markets.

Book Value

The value at which an asset is carried on the accounting records of a company. There are various book values, such as depreciated value, acquisition value, and so forth.

Breakeven

The financial point at which there is no loss or gain from operating a business, as the income and expenses are equal.

Brokerage

The business of a broker. In dentistry, the broker represents buyers and sellers in the transaction of a sale or acquisition of a practice. The broker will determine the value of the practice, lists the practices, and so forth. There are different types of brokers who provide either a very limited or a very rich array of services to coordinate and arrange a contract between two parties.

Budget

An itemized summary of probable income and expenses for a specified period of time.

Business Owner's Policy

Combination property and business interruption policy, usually written for small- and medium-size businesses, to cover expenses (1) resulting from damage or destruction of business property or (2) when actions or nonactions of the business's representatives result in bodily injury or property damage to (an)other individual(s).

Buyer Patient Letter

A letter sent by the buyer to the patients of a newly purchased practice in which the buying doctor introduces him/herself to the community.

Buyer Questionnaire/Profile

A form used by brokerage agencies to ascertain what type of practice the buyer is looking for and to obtain references and acquaint the broker with the buyer. It is often the first step in pre-qualifying the buyer.

Buyer Representation

The agency relationship in which the broker owes all fiduciary responsibility to the buyer. The broker works on behalf of the buyer to the best of their professional ability. The broker can work to find a practice for the buyer as well as to investigate practices brought to the broker by the buyer for consideration of purchase.

Buy—Sell Agreement

See **Asset Purchase Agreement**

C

C Corporation

A business that elects to be taxed as a corporation. The C corporation pays federal and state income taxes on earnings. When the earnings are distributed to the share-holders as dividends, this income is subject to another round of taxation (shareholder's income). Essentially, the C corporations' earnings are taxed twice. In contrast, the S corporation's earnings are taxed only once.

Capital

Cash or other resources available for use in producing wealth.

Capital Contribution

A contribution of funds or property to the capital of a business by a partner, owner, or shareholder. Under the Internal Revenue Code, a capital contribution is gener-ally excluded from a company's gross income, unless it is a loan from a shareholder that the company is released from repaying.

Capitalization of Excess Earnings

A method of valuation of a business that is frequently considered the state of the art in the appraisal profession. The method is a hybrid that combines cost and income approaches and takes into consideration the historical income and expenses of the business and adjusts the ex-penses and applies a capitalization (most easily defined as a risk rate) to determine value.

Capitalization Rate (Cap Rate)

The rate at which one would discount future income to determine current value. It can also be said to be the risk rate applicable to a given business. Not all businesses in a given profession will have the same cap rate. It is influenced by area, profession, and the strength or weaknesses of a given business.

Capitation Plan

The practice of dentistry financed by a set fee per person per given period of time. A form of contracted dental care, usually by a corporation, institution, or other group. A system by which the contracting dental professional assuming the financial risk is compensated at a fixed per capita rate, usually on specific, predetermined dental services as appropriate and necessary to eligible subscribers.

Cash Flow

Arrived at by subtracting the expenses to operate a business from the gross income of that business.

Cash Flow Lender

Lenders who loan money to purchase a business based on the strength of the cash flow of the target combined with the strength of the credit history and the debt-to-equity ratio of the buyer.

Cash Flow Projection

See **Pro forma**

Certified Financial Planner (CFP)

A title conveyed by the International Board of Standards and Practices for Certified Financial Planners. A Certified Financial Planner must pass a series of exams and enroll in ongoing education classes. Knowledge of estate planning, tax preparation, insurance, and investing is required.

Claims Made Policy

Claims made policies are policies commonly associated with professional liability policies, such as Directors & Officers, Employment Practices Liability, and other miscellaneous professional liability policies, including Lawyers Professional Liability.

Closing Documents

A group of documents required by the various federal, state, local and professional agencies to legally consummate a business sale/ acquisition.

8594

The form required by the IRS that defines the various tax classes for tangible and intangible assets in a sale/ acquisition transaction.

State letter

Letter signed by parties to a transaction that is sent to the State Board of Dentistry to inform them of the transfer of a practice.

Personal closing statement

The financial breakdown of the buyer's purchase price or the seller's sale proceeds that reflects the amounts to be paid to the owner outside of a corporation

Corporate closing statement

The financial breakdown of the buyer's purchase price or the seller's sale proceeds that reflects the amounts to be paid to the seller's corporation.

Real estate closing statement
The financial breakdown of the buyer's purchase price or the seller's sale proceeds that reflects the amounts to be paid. This will also reflect title insurance, filing fees, and so forth.

Accounts receivable closing statement
The financial breakdown of the buyer's purchase price or the seller's sale proceeds that reflects the amounts to be paid for the acquisition of the monies owed to the seller by his patients. This would reflect an aging schedule and the discounts applied to the various categories.

Collateral
Assets pledged to secure a loan.

Collateralized Lender
Lenders who loan money to purchase a business based on the concept of the buyer pledging assets against the money borrowed.

Collection Percentage
The amount of money collected for services rendered divided by the total amount of production.

Collections
Money paid by patients for services.

Commission
The fee charged by a broker for services performed on behalf of a customer.

Comparable Value

A measurement of worth based on the selling price of a similar business property.

Comparables

Comparables (or Comps) refers to data about properties that are comparable in type and size to those of interest to a buyer or to the property a seller wishes to list. This data can be past sold property prices and information or list prices and data on current listings.

Compound Interest

Interest computed on the sum of the original principal and its accrued interest.

Confidentiality Agreement/Form

A form used by brokers to ensure that prospective buyers keep all information confidential as it relates to any practice(s) they investigate. As the information is very sensitive and confidential in nature, it is imperative that name, location, and financial data not be disclosed as it could negatively impact the value of a practice.

Consulting

Use of a specialist advisor in practice management. There is a broad range of consultants who vary in the depth of services and knowledge.

Contract Planning Meeting

The meeting held by some companies between the buyer and seller in which an outline is followed that deals with all the elements in a purchase agreement for the practice, the Accounts Receivable, and if applicable, the related dental building. There is a memo generated from the meeting that goes to the attorneys to draft the contracts.

Covenant Not to Compete (Covenant or Restrictive Covenant)

This is a contract signed between a host doctor and associate that defines the terms of employment in which the associate agrees not to practice dentistry or solicit the patients or staff of a practice for a given time period and within a given mile radius. The covenant generally begins at the termination of the employment.

Credit

The confidence in a purchaser's or borrower's ability and intention to pay for goods, services or loans without immediate payment but rather with payment based upon an agreement between the parties for a promise of future repayment.

Credit Authorization

The signed form that provides permission to credit reporting agencies to release the signed individual's credit history to a third party.

Credit Rating

An estimate of the amount of credit that can be extended to an individual or business without undue risk, based upon historical performance with credit cards or borrowing that is rated by various credit agencies.

Credit Report

A loan and bill payment history kept by a credit bureau and used by financial institutions and other potential creditors to determine the likelihood a future debt will be repaid.

Creditor

A person, financial institution, or other business that lends money.

Curriculum Vitae

A curriculum vitae is a written description of your work experience, educational background, and skills. Also called a CV, or simply a vitae, it is more detailed than a resume and is commonly used by those looking for work.

D

DBA

Acronym for Doing Business As.

Debit

Charges to an account.

Debt

Money owed. Also known as a liability.

Debt Service

The amount of money that is owed to a lender for the purchase of a business. It is comprised of the periodic payment of the principal and interest on the loan.

Delayed Sale

The sale of a business that is organized and defined to take place at a later date. The price, terms, and contracts are all completed with an effective date that could be triggered by a specific event or on a specific date.

Depreciation

A noncash expense that reduces the value of an asset as a result of wear and tear, age, or obsolescence. Most assets lose their value over time (in other words, they depreciate), and must be replaced once the end of their useful life is reached.

Derivative

A financial instrument whose characteristics and value depend upon the characteristics and value of an underlier, typically a commodity, bond, equity, or currency.

Option

The right, but not the obligation, to buy (for a call option) or sell (for a put option) a specific amount of a given stock, commodity, currency, index, or debt, at a specified price (the strike price) during a specified period of time.

Futures

A standardized, transferable, exchange-traded contract that requires delivery of a commodity, bond, currency, or stock index, at a specified price, on a specified future date. Unlike options, futures convey an obligation to buy.

Disability Insurance

Insurance policy that pays benefits in the event that the policyholder becomes incapable of working.

Discretionary Income

The amount of an individual's income available for spending after the essentials (such as food, clothing, and shelter) have been taken care of.

Distress Sale

The sale of a business that has a forced sale time frame due to various circumstances such as death or disability of the owner, loss of lease, loss of license, or other events would prevent the owner from continuing in business. This type of sale generally results in a considerably lower sale price.

Diversification

The distribution of investments among several market sectors to lessen the risk of loss.

Dividend

A payment by a corporation to its stockholders, usually representing a share in the company's earnings.

Dual Representation

This practice is *illegal* in the state of Florida. Both buyer and seller in a transaction are represented by the same agent. This can result in a conflict of interest for the parties. The agent cannot give 100% of fiduciary responsibility to either party.

Due Diligence

The process of investigation performed by potential buyers of a business (practice), including items such as an examination/investigation of the systems, patient records, production, net income, employees, and the verification of the material facts to ascertain the veracity of the materials presented for the purchase.

E

Earn Out

Refers to an additional payment in a merger or acquisition that is not part of the original acquisition cost, which is based on the acquired company's future earnings relative to a level determined by the merger agreement.

Earning Requirements

The amount of money that a prospective purchaser needs to support their household budget and service debt on school loans prior to the debt of a practice.

Emergency Patient

A patient seen in a practice only for treatment to resolve a specific problem. This is not a patient of record who has been seen in the practice for regular hygiene or operative treatment, but a one-time visit to resolve an emergency appointment, generally to relieve pain.

Employment Agreement or Associate Agreement

The contractual agreement between a host doctor and a doctor employed to treat patients of the host doctor's practice. It will define the terms and expectations of the employment.

An employment agreement may also be used for employees of a practice to define expectations of employment in return for the agreed-upon pay rate and schedule.

Entrepreneur

A person who has possession over a company, enterprise, or venture, and assumes significant accountability for the inherent risks and outcome.

Environmental Phase I

A proscribed site analysis that reviews historical records, performed by certified individuals, that shows a succession of ownership and uses of the specific property and properties surrounding the target property, the confluence of water, and indications of further testing for risk of ground or water contamination. This was considered essential at one time, as it showed the status of the property at the time of transfer of ownership.

Escrow (as part of purchase offer)

Monies placed in to an escrow account, which is, by definition, a noninterest bearing account, sometimes referred to as a trust account, generally supervised by brokers or attorneys to hold the funds placed there as part of a contractual agreement until certain criteria are met.

Estimated Taxes

The method used to pay tax on income that is not subject to withholding. This includes income from self-employment. Estimated tax is used to pay income tax and self-employment tax, as well as other taxes and amounts reported on your tax return. If you do not pay enough through withholding or estimated tax payments, you may be charged a penalty. If you do not pay enough by the due date of each payment period, you may be charged a penalty even if you are due a refund when you file your tax return.

Equity
Ownership interest in an asset after liabilities are deducted.

F

Face Value
The nominal value or dollar value of a security stated by the issuer. For stocks, it is the original cost of the stock shown on the certificate. For bonds, it is the amount paid to the holder at maturity (generally $1,000). Also known as "par value" or simply "par."

Fair Market Value
Defined by the IRS as ".. the price at which the property would change hands between a willing buyer and a willing seller when the former is not under any compulsion to buy and the latter is not under any compulsion to sell, both parties having reasonable knowledge of relevant facts" (*Revenue Ruling 59-60 (1959-2 C.B. 237)*).

Federal Deposit Insurance Corporation

A federal chartered corporation that insures bank deposits up to $250,000 through December 31, 2009. After this date, bank deposits will be insured up to $100,000.

Fee Increases

The incremental increase of procedural fees for treatment that is generally increased every one to two years. These increases may coincide with the fees increases set by the insurance industry.

Fee Schedule

The cost of services for dental treatment rendered to patients that is defined individually by each doctor. Each procedure is broken down by a code. The code is universally accepted by the American Dental Association.

FICA Tax

The Federal Insurance Contributions Act (FICA) tax is a United States payroll (or employment) tax imposed by the federal government on both employees and employers to fund Social Security and Medicare—federal programs that provide benefits for retirees, the disabled, and children of deceased workers. Social Security benefits include old-age, survivors, and disability insurance (OASDI).

Fiduciary

An individual, corporation, or association holding assets for another party, often with the legal authority and duty to make decisions regarding financial matters on behalf of the other party.

Financing Fee

The fee a lender charges to originate a loan. The fee is based on a percentage of the loan amount. One point is equivalent to 1%.

Fixed Asset

A long-term tangible piece of property that a firm owns and uses in the production of its income and is not expected to be consumed or converted into cash any sooner than at least one year's time.

Fixed Income

A security that pays a specific interest rate, such as a bond, money market instrument, or preferred stock.

CD

Certificate of Deposit. Short- or medium-term, interest bearing, FDIC-insured debt instrument offered by banks and savings and loans. CDs offer higher rates of return than most comparable investments in exchange for tying up invested money for the duration of the certificate's maturity.

Money Market Fund

An open-end mutual fund invests only in money markets. Unlike bank accounts and money market accounts, most deposits are not FDIC insured, but the risk is extremely low.

Guaranteed Investment Contract

Debt instrument issued by an insurance company, usually in a large denomination, and often bought for retirement plans. The interest rate paid is guaranteed, but the principal is not.

Bond
A debt instrument issued for a period of more than one year with the purpose of raising capital by borrowing. The federal government, states, cities, corporations, and many other types of institutions sell bonds. Generally, a bond is a promise to repay the principal along with interest (coupons) on a specified date (maturity).

Municipal bond
Bond issued by a state, city, or local government. Municipalities issue bonds to raise capital for their day-to-day activities and for specific projects that they might be undertaking (usually pertaining to development of local infrastructure such as roads, sewerage, hospitals, etc). Interest on municipal bonds is generally exempt from federal tax. Municipal bonds usually come in $5,000 par values and usually require a minimum investment of $25,000 in order to get the best price.

General Obligation Bond
Type of municipal bond backed by the full faith and credit of the government entity that issues it.

Revenue Bond
Bond issued by a municipality to finance a specific public works project and supported by the revenues of that project. Also called municipal revenue bond.

Corporate Bond
A type of bond issued by a corporation. Corporate bonds often pay higher rates than government or municipal bonds because they tend to be riskier. The bond holder receives interest payments (yield) and the principal, usually $1000, is repaid on a fixed maturity date (bonds can mature anywhere between one to thirty years).

High Yield
Description of investments with high rates of return.

Government Bond
A bond sold by the U.S. government.

Treasury Bill
A negotiable debt obligation issued by the U.S. government and backed by its full faith and credit, having a maturity of one year or less. Exempt from state and local taxes.

Treasury Note
A negotiable debt obligation issued by the U.S. government and backed by its full faith and credit, having a maturity of between one and seven years.

Treasury Bond
A negotiable, coupon-bearing debt obligation issued by the U.S. government and backed by its full faith and credit, having a maturity of more than seven years. Interest is paid semi-annually. Treasury bonds are exempt from state and local taxes.

TIPS
Treasury Inflation-Protected Security. A security that is identical to a treasury bond except that principal and coupon payments are adjusted to eliminate the effects of inflation.

Savings Bond
A registered, noncallable, nontransferable bond issued by the U.S. government and backed by its full faith and credit. Savings bonds are nonmarketable, meaning that they cannot be bought and sold after they are purchased from the government; therefore, there is no secondary market for savings bonds.

Floor Plan
Diagram of a facility. In the dental profession, it would show the layout of operatories, business areas, patient reception, storage, mechanical areas, lab, sterilization, restrooms, private office, lounge, and so forth. The plan should show entrance and egress to the facility, each room, and the dimensions.

G

Geo Site Search or Demographic Report
A report that shows the breakdown in given areas by population, age, income, zip code, education, and so forth.

Geographical Preference

Any given area that a buyer defines as a location in which he or she would like to practice. The wider the preferential area, the more likely one is to find a practice.

Goodwill

An intangible asset valued according to the advantage or reputation a business has acquired (over and above its tangible assets).

Guaranteed Payments to a Partner

Payments to individual partners for services rendered or for use of capital not based on the partner's share of partnership income. Guaranteed payments to partners are deducted from partnership income before determining partnership profit or loss. Guaranteed payments are generally subject to self-employment tax on the recipient's individual return. If the partnership agreement states a partner is to receive a minimum payment, the guaranteed payment is the amount by which the minimum payment is more than the partner's distributive share of income, before taking into account the minimum payment. Guaranteed payments can cause a partnership loss. The partner(s) who receives the guaranteed payment reports the full amount as ordinary income. The partner also reports his or her distributive share of the partnership loss.

H

HIPAA

Acronym that stands for the Health Insurance Portability and Accountability Act, a U.S. law designed to provide privacy standards to protect patients' medical records and other health information provided to health plans, doctors, hospitals, and other health care providers.

I

Indemnity Insurance Plans

An indemnity plan reimburses you for your medical expenses, regardless of who provides the service. In some situations/types of coverage, this amount may be limited. The coverage offered by most insurers is in the form of an indemnity plan.

Industrial Bond

A financial instrument issued by businesses to fund expansion or acquisition.

Installment Plan

A plan requiring a borrower to make payments at specified intervals during the life of a loan.

Insurance

Coverage by contract whereby one party agrees to indemnify or guarantee another against loss by a specified event or peril.

Intangible Asset
A nonphysical claim to future value or benefits.

Interest
A fee for the use of money over time. Also, money earned on a savings account.

Interest rate
The percentage charged for a loan. Also, the percentage paid on a savings account or bond.

Investing
The act of using money to make more money.

Investor
A person, organization, corporation, or other entity that acquires ownership in an investment, assuming risk of loss in exchange of anticipated returns.

K

Keogh Plan
A type of tax deferred retirement plan for the self employed.

L

Labs

The professional services to create the crown and bridge services for dental restorations. This overhead expense should be 8–12% of gross production.

Lease Agreements

A document under which a landlord and tenant set forth the rights and obligations of each party with respect to an apartment, rental unit, or other real property owned by the landlord and used by the tenant. An instrument conveying the possession of real property for a fixed period of time in consideration of the payment of rent.

Leasehold Improvements

Upgrading made by a lessee to leased property. Examples are paneling, wallpapering, and cabinetry affixed to the walls. These improvements revert to the lessor at the expiration of the lease term.

Lender Loan Proposal

The loan format proposed by the lender to a specific borrower on a specific practice. This is not the loan commitment, merely the loan structure proposed by a lender in the event the lender approves the loan through its underwriters.

Lender's Letter of Commitment, Loan Approval

The commitment to a buyer to lend funds from a specific lender, for a specific practice after it has been approved by the underwriters of the lender.

Letter of Intent, Commitment Letter or Purchase Offer, Buyer's Letter of Intent

Formalized document signed by prospective purchaser to make clear the desire to purchase and the price and terms of the offer. An accepted offer is signed by the seller as well. This is *not* the detailed purchase agreement.

Letter of Value/Letter of Appraisal

An abbreviated report for a market analysis that illustrates how the range of values was derived and designates a target price of the specified practice.

Leverage

The ability to use a small amount of money to attract other funds, including loans, grants, and equity investments.

Liability

Money owed. Also known as debt.

Lien

The right to retain the lawful possession of the property of another until the owner fulfills a legal duty to the person holding the property, such as the payment of lawful charges for work done on the property. A mortgage is a common lien.

Lien Search

This is also called a UCC (Uniform Commercial Code) Search. The purpose of this search is to determine outstanding debts, in what amounts, and held by whom that must be cleared to enable the buyer to obtain clear title to the practice/property.

Life Insurance

Insurance that guarantees a specific sum of money to a designated beneficiary upon the death of the insured or to the insured if he or she lives beyond a certain age.

Line of Credit

An arrangement in which a bank or vendor extends a specified amount of unsecured credit to a specified borrower for a specified time period at a given rate of interest.

Liquidity

The ease with which an investment can be converted into cash.

LLC

Limited Liability Company. A type of company, authorized only in certain states, whose owners and managers receive the limited liability without having to conform to corporation restrictions.

Loan Proposal

The complete document package compiling financial information on both the practice and the buyer/borrower of which the loan request is a part.

Loan Request

This is the formalized request for funding of a dental acquisition. It could include additional funds for purchasing equipment, software, purchasing accounts receivable and even money to buy a building.

Long-term Liability
Recorded on the balance sheet, a company's liabilities for leases, bond repayments, and other items due in more than one year.

M

Management Fee
The fee paid to a company for managing an investment portfolio.

Marginal Tax Rate
The amount of tax paid on an additional dollar of income. As income rises, so does the tax rate.

Market Value
The amount of money a seller can expect to receive on the open market for merchandise, services, or securities.

Matching Concept
The accounting principle that requires the recognition of all costs that are associated with the generation of the revenue reported in the income statement.

Maturity
The time when a note, bond, or other investment comes due for payment to investors.

Medicare Tax

A tax deducted from employees' paychecks that goes to pay for medical benefits for people over 65 years of age. Medicare tax is paid by both employee and employer.

N

Net Worth

The difference between a person's total assets and total liabilities.

New Patients

New patients in a practice are defined as those patients who join the practice to receive treatment in an ongoing basis for both hygiene and operative treatment. These are not emergency patients who are seen merely for palliative care.

Nondisclosure Form or Confidentiality Form

A form used by brokers to assure that prospective buyers keep all information confidential relating to any practice(s) they investigate. Because the information is very sensitive and confidential in nature, it is imperative that name, location, and financial data not be disclosed, as it could negatively impact the value of a practice.

Nonsolicitation Agreement

This may also be called a nonsolicitation agreement. It is an agreement that generally binds a doctor not to solicit the patients or staff from a given practice. The normal time that this is applicable is in a sale/acquisition or as a portion of an associate noncompete contract.

O

Occurrence Policy

Affords protection to the insured against any event described in the policy that occurred during the policy period, regardless of how long after expiration of the policy period the claim may arise.

Operating Agreement for Joint Owners of a Practice

A contractual agreement between joint owners of a practice that defines the manner in which the practice management and administrative responsibilities will be divided, profit will be split, equipment and supplies will be purchased, conflict resolution, employee issues and partner withdrawal, and so forth will be dealt with. A strong and thorough agreement can forestall many internal conflicts.

Operating Plan

Short term, highly detailed plan formulated generally by junior or departmental managers to achieve tactical objectives. Also called Operational Plan.

Overhead

The operating expenses of a business, including the costs of rent, utilities, interior decoration, and taxes, exclusive of labor and materials.

Overhead Percentage

Ratio between direct labor and overhead expenses. This percentage is used to allocate overhead expenses proportionately to direct labor dollars billed to customers.

Owner's Compensation

Cash and noncash (*see* **Personal Perks**) compensation for the practice owner.

Owner's Draw

The amount the owner draws from the practice on a monthly basis. This is based upon the owner's financial needs and the cash-flow of the practice.

P

Par Value

The value imprinted on a security, such as a stock certificate or bond, used to calculate a payment, such as a dividend or interest; face value. Also called nominal value.

Parity

Equality, as in amount, status, or value.

Participation Agreement

The contracts reference the goals of the parties, identify the process, define the professionals' roles, and set forth the codes of conduct by which the participants will be guided during the process.

Partnership

The Uniform Partnership Act defines a partnership as "an association of two or more persons to carry on as co-owners of a business for profit."

Personal Budget Form

A form that facilitates and monitors monthly income and expenditures. Lenders will require that this form be a part of the loan request package.

Personal Financial Statement/Form

A form that defines the assets and liabilities of an individual. Lenders will require that this form be a part of the loan request package.

Personal Perks

Expenses that are allowable and can be charged through the practice and may be discretionary to another operator. An example of this would be the type of automobile, cell phones, travel as part of a continuing education seminar, and so forth.

PLLC

Professional corporations and professional limited liability companies (PLLCs) are corporations and limited liability companies organized for the purpose of providing professional services.

Pooled Fund

Any fund in which multiple investors contribute assets and hold them as a group.

Mutual fund

An open-ended fund operated by an investment company that raises money from shareholders and invests in a group of assets, in accordance with a stated set of objectives.

Open-end fund

A fund operated by an investment company that raises money from shareholders and invests in a group of assets, in accordance with a stated set of objectives. Open-end funds raise money by selling shares of the fund to the public, much like any other type of company, which can sell stock in itself to the public.

Closed-end fund

A fund with a fixed number of shares outstanding, and one that does not redeem shares the way a typical mutual fund does. Closed-end funds behave more like stock than open-end funds: closed-end funds issue a fixed number of shares to the public in an initial public offering, after which time shares in the fund are bought and sold on a stock exchange, and they are not obligated to issue new shares or redeem outstanding shares as open-end funds are.

No-load fund

A mutual fund that doesn't impose a sales or redemption charge, selling and redeeming its shares at net asset value. Opposite of load fund.

Hedge fund

A fund, usually used by wealthy individuals and institutions, that is allowed to use aggressive strategies unavailable to mutual funds, including selling short, leverage, program trading, swaps, arbitrage, and derivatives. Hedge funds are exempt from many of the rules and regulations governing other mutual funds, which allows them to accomplish aggressive investing goals.

Exchange traded fund (ETF)

A fund that tracks an index but can be traded like a stock. ETFs always bundle together the securities that are in an index; they never track actively managed mutual fund portfolios (because most actively managed funds only disclose their holdings a few times a year, so the ETF would not know when to adjust its holdings most of the time).

Practice Broker

A practice broker is a person or firm who/ acts as an intermediary between sellers and buyers of dental practices.

Practice Continuation Agreement

Contractual agreement between the owner of a practice and other doctors who will continue to operate the practice until a buyer can be found, or for a specified time frame, in the event the owner is disabled or passes away. Frequently, this agreement will be part of an associate employment agreement.

Practice Management Consultant

An individual with specialized skills and experience with dental practices who can guide a practitioner in the areas of creating a mission statement, scheduling, production, overhead expenses, staff management, verbal skills, collections, adjustments, fee assessment, and so forth.

Pre-tax

Before taxes have been deducted.

Prime Rate

The prime rate of interest is a rate of interest that serves as a benchmark for most other loans in a country.

Principal

The outstanding balance owed on a debt, excluding interest.

Pro forma

A twelve to twenty-four-month calculation of income and expenses based upon the historical performance of a given business and then applying the manner in which a given new owner would run the same business. Note: ADS Florida only provides this as an estimation of income and expenses for the first year after a purchase.

Production

In dental practices, the billable procedures (generally, by hour) that a practice produces.

Production by Procedure Report

This report calculates production as a total of different procedures, such as crowns, bridges, and so forth.

Professional Liability Insurance

Professional liability insurance, also called Professional Indemnity Insurance, protects professional practitioners such as architects, lawyers, physicians, and accountants against potential negligence claims made by their patients/clients.

Profit Sharing Plan

Plans that are available for employees to invest in for their retirement, such as 401Ks.

Profit Sharing Plan/401k

A deferred contribution plan set up by an employer that allows employees to deduct a portion of their salary from their paycheck to be set aside for retirement on a pretax basis.

Promissory Note

A promissory note is a contract that involves an unconditional promise by one party to pay money to another party according to the terms of the agreement.

Proprietorship (Sole)

A business owned and operated by an individual.

Proration

To allocate between two or more parties, the proportionate share of each. For example, the payment of property taxes or insurance premiums may be prorated between buyer and seller.

Prospectus

A report that describes a practice. It may include a letter of value or appraisal report, business tax returns, production, collection, production by procedure reports, aged accounts receivable, staff position, wages, benefits, bonus program, equipment appraisal, lease of building appraisal, demographic report, and fee schedule. This report may be distributed to prospective buyers.

Proxy

A written authorization given by a shareholder for someone else, usually the company's management, to cast his or her vote at a shareholder meeting or at another time.

Purchase Offer

An offer to purchase a practice brought forward by a prospective buyer.

Purchase Agreement

A legal agreement detailing a sale of property, including price and terms.

Q

Qualified Intermediary

Substitutes for or on behalf of the exchanger as the seller or buyer, depending on which side of the transaction you are on, and holds the net sales proceeds from the sale of the relinquished property in a segregated account.

Quote

The highest bid or lowest ask price available on a security at any given time.

R

Record Count

The count made of active patients in a practice. This count can be either digital or physical paper charts. The total number of charts is determined, and then the active patients are determined. Historically, computer counts reports have been 8%–20% higher than a physical record count of the same patient base. This is dependent on the software.

Real Estate Closing Fees

Closing costs are everything outside of the purchase price that a buyer pays to complete a real estate transaction. For a seller, closing costs are all the fees, except liens or encumbrances, that are deducted from the purchase price. Fees range from those paid to title, escrow, or lawyers; documentary transfer tax; city/county transfer or property taxes; credit reports; appraisal; recording or notary fees; real estate commissions; inspections; loan fees, such as points; and prepaid interest.

Origination fees
The fee charged by the lender for originating a loan. This fee is usually calculated in the form of points and paid at closing.

Recording fees
Fees charged by the county to record the property deed in the public record and any other documents required to clear title. Fees are generally charged by the page.

Recall Percentage
The percentage of the patient base in a practice that come to the practice on a biannual basis for their hygiene re-care appointments. This percentage should be 85% or above.

References
Contacts that an individual seeking employment lists as possible to provide character, volunteer experience, and/or work or insights.

Clinical
References that refer to a candidate's abilities as they apply to clinical performance.

Personal
References that are provided by individuals who can speak to the character of a candidate over a span of time.

Financial

This could be from a banker, investment advisor or be in the form of a current (six months or less) credit report from all three credit reporting agencies.

REIT

Real Estate Investment Trust. A corporation or trust that uses the pooled capital of many investors to purchase and manage income property (equity REIT) and/or mortgage loans (mortgage REIT). REITs are traded on major exchanges just like stocks. They are also granted special tax considerations. REITs offer several benefits over actually owning properties. First, they are highly liquid, unlike traditional real estate. Second, REITs enable sharing in nonresidential properties as well, such as hotels, malls, and other commercial or industrial properties. Third, there's no minimum investment with REITs. REITs do not necessarily increase and decrease in value along with the broader market. However, they pay yields in the form of dividends no matter how the shares perform. REITs can be valued based upon fundamental measures, similar to the valuation of stocks, but different numbers tend to be important for REITs than for stocks.

Restrictive Covenant

An agreement included in a deed to real property that the buyer (grantee) will be limited as to the future use of the property. *See* **Covenant Not to Compete**

Retirement Plans

There are various types of retirement plans that provide income during the years after one has completed one's career work life. Retirement plans all work essentially by the mechanism of an individual placing defined amounts of money monthly, quarterly or annually in a given plan that earns interest and may defer taxes until the time the money is withdrawn incrementally. Forms of retirement are Individual Retirement Accounts (IRAs), qualified retirement plans, safe harbor plans, 401, 403b, Simple Plans, SEP Keogh, ESOP, and so forth.

Qualified retirement plan
A plan that meets the requirements of Internal Revenue Code Section 401(a) and the Employee Retirement Income Security Act of 1974 (ERISA) and is thus eligible for favorable tax treatment. These plans offer several tax benefits: they allow employers to deduct annual allowable contributions for each participant, contributions and earnings on those contributions are tax-deferred until withdrawn for each participant, and some of the taxes can be deferred even further through a transfer into a different type of IRA.

ERISA
Employee Retirement Income Security Act of 1974. The federal law established legal guidelines for private pension plan administration and investment practices.

Defined contribution plan
A company retirement plan, such as a 401 (k) plan or 403(b) plan, in which the employee elects to defer some amount of his or her salary into the plan and bears the investment risk.

Profit-sharing
An arrangement in which an employer shares some of its profits with its employees.

401(k) plan
A defined contribution plan offered by a corporation to its employees, which allows employees to set aside tax-deferred income for retirement purposes; in some cases, employers will match their contribution dollar-for-dollar. The name 401 (k) comes from the IRS section describing the program.

Roth 401(k)
A contribution-based retirement account, which combines features of the traditional Roth IRA and 401(k) plan accounts. The Roth 40l(k) contains many benefits for employees, such as being able to contribute post-tax money.

Defined benefit plan
A company retirement plan, such as a pension plan, in which a retired employee receives a specific amount based on salary history and years of service, and in which the employer bears the investment risk. Contributions may be made by the employee, the employer, or both.

Savings Incentive Match Plan for Employees (SIMPLE)
A retirement plan sponsored by companies with fewer than one hundred employees, which is attractive for employers because it avoids some of the administra-

tive fees and paperwork of plans such as a 401 (k) plan. A SIMPLE plan may be structured as a 401 (k).

SEP plan

A retirement program for self-employed people or owners of companies with less than twenty-five employees, allowing them to defer taxes on investments intended for retirement. This plan allows employers to contribute on behalf of eligible employees, and all contributions are tax-deductible as a business expense and can be integrated with Social Security contributions. In addition, there is no minimum contribution requirement.

Individual Retirement Account

A type of retirement plan offered by banks, brokerage firms, and insurance companies to which investors can contribute each year on a tax-deferred basis.

Traditional IRA

Individual Retirement Account. A tax-deferred retirement account for an individual that permits individuals to set aside money each year, with earnings tax-deferred until withdrawals begin at age 59½ or later (or earlier, with a 10% penalty). IRAs can be established at a bank, mutual fund, or brokerage. Only those who do not participate in a pension plan at work or who do participate and meet certain income guidelines can make deductible contributions to an IRA. All others can make contributions to an IRA on a nondeductible basis.

Roth IRA

A new type of IRA, established in the Taxpayer Relief Act of 1997, which allows taxpayers, subject to certain income limits, to save for retirement while allowing the savings to grow tax-free. Taxes are paid on contributions, but withdrawals, subject to certain rules, are not taxed at all.

Retirement Sale

The sale of a practice when the seller has completed their professional career and leaves the practice. There may be a brief period where the seller completes work in progress, such as delivering crowns or bridges.

Return

The profit made on an investment. Also known as return on investment.

Risk

The quantifiable likelihood of loss or less-than-expected returns.

S

S Corporation

A form of corporation, allowed by the IRS for most companies with seventy-five or fewer shareholders, that enables the company to enjoy the benefits of incorporation but be taxed as if it were a partnership. Also called Subchapter S Corporation.

Scheduling
The system utilized to set patient visits to the office for hygiene or operative treatment in individual operatories to be seen by a given doctor or hygienist.

Block
A type of scheduling in which the doctor has fewer patients per day for a longer period of time, as certain types of procedures are segregated timewise. This is intended to result in a more profitable day due to less time wasted, switching from operatory to operatory for smaller procedures. It also allows for the major procedures on a daily basis with smaller procedures scheduled around to fill the day.

Linear
Method whereby doctor/hygienist treats one patient until he or she has completed that treatment before moving on to another patient in another operatory.

Overlapping
Doctor and assistant work with patients in two or more operatories rotating between them as the treatment requires. As an example, the doctor may be in operatory one to give an injection while an assistant is in operatory two, preparing an impression material for the doctor to take the impression while the patient in operatory one is numbing up.

Short Term Liability
Obligations that have to be satisfied in one to five years.

Showing

Refers to the on-site visit of a practice by prospective purchaser in which he or she is accompanied by a representing broker. The prospective purchaser should be free to audit charts, review systems, equipment, tour facility, and interview the seller.

Space Sharing Arrangement

Either a contractual or informal arrangement where two doctors share the same clinical facility. Both can be on the lease, or one holds the lease and the other doctor sublets. There are various forms that are either very integrated or separate to a great degree. Some share employees, equipment, and computers. Others have separate operatories with their own equipment, hardware, and software and share only physical space. To be done efficiently and not negatively impact a future sale, the arrangement should be very well thought out, formalized by a legal and binding contract with specific criteria.

Stock

An instrument that signifies an ownership position (called equity) in a corporation and represents a claim on its proportional share in the corporation's assets and profits. Ownership in the company is determined by the number of shares a person owns divided by the total number of shares outstanding. Most stock also provides voting rights, which give shareholders a proportional vote in certain corporate decisions. Only a certain type of company, called a corporation, has stock; other types of companies such as sale proprietorships and limited partnerships do not issue stock.

Common stock
Securities representing equity ownership in a corporation, providing voting rights. and entitling the holder to a share of the company's success through dividends and/or capital appreciation.

Preferred stock
Capital stock that provides a specific dividend paid before any dividends are paid to common stockholders and takes precedence over common stock in the event of a liquidation. The main benefit to owning preferred stock is that the investor has a greater claim on the company's assets than common stockholders.

Stock Market
General term for the organized trading of stocks through exchanges and over-the-counter.

NYSE
New York Stock Exchange. The largest stock exchange in the United States, located on Wall Street in New York City. The NYSE is responsible for setting policy, supervising member activities, listing securities, overseeing the transfer of member seats, and evaluating applicants. Of the exchanges, the NYSE has the most stringent set of requirements in place for the companies whose stocks it lists, and even meeting these requirements is not a guarantee that the NYSE will list the company. Also called Big Board.

NASDAQ
A computerized system established by the NASD to facilitate trading by providing broker/dealers with current bid and ask price quotes on over-the-counter stocks and some listed stocks. Unlike the Amex and the NYSE, the NASDAQ (once an acronym for the National Association of Securities Dealers Automated Quotation system) does not have a physical trading floor that brings together buyers and sellers. Instead, all trading on the NASDAQ exchange is done over a network of computers and telephones. Also, the NASDAQ does not employ market specialists to buy unfilled orders like the NYSE does. Orders for stock are sent out electronically on the NASDAQ, where market makers list their buy and sell prices. Once a price is agreed upon, the transaction is executed electronically.

Over the counter (OTC)
A market for buying and selling stock between broker dealers over the telephone.

Stock Sale
Sale of shares in a company.

Stockholder
One who owns shares of stock in a corporation or mutual fund.

Supplies
Items and materials that are needed to operate and perform either business or clinical procedures.

Office

Items such as paper, ink, toners, charts, forms, paper clips, rubber bands, letterhead, envelopes, and so forth required to perform the business operation of a practice.

Dental

An array of items used in providing dental treatment to patients. It ranges from neck bibs to burrs. It can be impression material, occlusion paper, resins, and so forth.

General

Items necessary for the esthetic or hygienic operation of a business enterprise such as air freshener, hand towels, cleaning supplies, flowers, or other such items.

T

Taxes

Payroll

Tax payments automatically taken out of an employee's wages by the employer and forwarded to the government. Payroll taxes generally refers to two kinds of taxes: Taxes that employers are required to withhold from employees' pay, also known as withholding, and taxes that are paid from the employer's own funds, which are directly related to employing a worker. These may be either fixed charges or proportionally linked to an employee's pay.

Personal property taxes
Taxes on auto license plates, equipment in a practice.

Real estate taxes
Taxes on a home or business property.

Quarterly estimates
When an individual is self-employed, there are no payroll taxes withheld from the paycheck. Therefore, the self-employed must pay taxes on a quarterly basis. These taxes are estimates based on the prior year's income.

Tax Credit
Tax credits may be characterized as either refundable or nonrefundable, or equivalently non-wastable or wastable. Refundable or non-wastable tax credits can reduce the tax owed below zero and result in a net payment to the taxpayer beyond their own payments into the tax system, appearing to be a moderate form of negative income tax.

Tax Deduction
An expense subtracted from adjusted gross income when calculating taxable income, such as for state and local taxes paid, charitable gifts, and certain types of interest payments.

Tax-deferred
Income whose taxes can be postponed until a later date. Examples include IRA, 401 (k), Keogh Plan, annuity, Savings Bond, and Employee Stock Ownership Plan.

Tax Entity

Person, partnership, organization, or business unit that has a legal existence, for which accounting records are kept, and about which financial statements are prepared.

Tax Qualified Retirement Plan

An employee benefit plan, such as a 401 (k), that defers taxation on both contributions and earnings until money is withdrawn.

1031 Tax Deferred Exchange

It is the last remaining tax shelter for real estate investment. IRC 1031 is part of the Internal Revenue Code that allows, under certain conditions, the taxpayer to defer paying the tax owed at the time of sale until some future date. The tax-deferred exchange is simply an exchange of the adjusted gain, or profit, for another property.

Term

Fixed period for which a loan, insurance policy, or bond is issued; a time or fixed deposit is made; or a contract lasts.

Term Life Insurance

Simplest and usually the cheapest type of life insurance that stays in effect for a specified period or until a certain age of the insured. It pays the face amount of the policy in case the insured dies within the coverage period (term) but pays nothing if he or she outlives it.

Terms

Provisions specified in a loan agreement.

Title Company

A company involved in examining and insuring title claims, usually for real estate on behalf of its customers.

Title Insurance

Insurance to protect a lender or owner against loss in the event of a property ownership dispute.

Trading

Buying and selling securities or commodities on a short-term basis, hoping to make quick profits. More generally, any buying and selling of securities or commodities.

Short sale

Borrowing a security (or commodity futures contract) from a broker and selling it, with the understanding that it must later be bought back (hopefully at a lower price) and returned to the broker. Short selling (or "selling short") is a technique used by investors who try to profit from the falling price of a stock. Short selling is a very risky technique. SEC rules allow investors to sell short only on an uptick or a zero-plus tick, to prevent "pool operators" from driving down a stock price through heavy shortselling, then buying the shares for a large profit.

Margin buying

A risky technique involving the purchase of securities with borrowed money, using the shares themselves as collateral. Usually done using a margin account at a brokerage, and subject to fairly strict SEC buying on margin regulations.

Transaction

The exchange of goods or services between a buyer and a seller.

Transition

The transfer of a dental practice from one dentist owner to another. This involves not only the financial aspect of the business sale, but also assisting the dentist and staff through all aspects of making the transition successful for the patients and staff.

Transition Seminar

A seminar that is presented by a transition specialist that presents an in-depth discussion of the procedures and provides information needed to successfully complete a dental practice sale transfer.

Triggering Event

A tangible or intangible barrier or occurrence that, once breached or met, causes another event to occur.

Turn Key Operation

In real estate, delivering a location that is ready for occupation.

U

UA 1027

In general, a person or business that acquires the organization, trade, business, or 75% or more of the assets of a business will be liable for unemployment taxes and interest due the government.

UCC

The Uniform Commercial Code (UCC or the Code) is one of a number of uniform acts that have been promulgated in conjunction with efforts to harmonize the law of sales and other commercial transactions in all states within the United States of America.

UCC Search

The Uniform Commercial Code Bureau files and maintains records on financial obligations (including IRS liens) incurred by individuals (in business as a sole proprietor), business entities, and corporations.

Unemployment Agency

From the seller (or other transferor) of the business at the time of the transfer, up to the reasonable value of the business minus any secured interest in assets. This is the form you must send in to transfer those obligations to the new owner.

U.S. Savings Bond

A contract representing a loan that an individual makes to the U.S. government. The government repays the loan after a set period of time with a set interest rate.

W

Whole Life Insurance

Life insurance that provides coverage for an individual's whole life, rather than a specified term. A savings component, called cash value or loan value, builds over time and can be used for wealth accumulation. Whole life is the most basic form of cash value life insurance.

Working Capital

Also known as net working capital. A financial metric that represents operating liquidity available to a business.

Worker's Compensation

A form of insurance that provides compensation medical care for employees who are injured in the course of employment, in exchange for mandatory relinquishment of the employee's right to sue his or her employer for the tort of negligence.

Y

Year-to-date (YTD)

Signifies that reported figures reflect the period from the start of the year until the indicated date.

Yield

The annual rate of return on an investment, expressed as a percentage.

Made in the USA
Lexington, KY
07 September 2016